Rousseau

The Sentiment of Existence

Rousseau is often portrayed as an educational and social reformer whose aim was to increase individual freedom. In this volume, the distinguished philosopher David Gauthier examines Rousseau's evolving notion of freedom, particularly in his later works, where he focuses on a single quest: Can freedom and the independent self be regained? Rousseau's first answer is given in *Emile*, where he seeks to create a self-sufficient individual, neither materia͘ or psychologically enslaved to others. His second a͘ es in the *Social Contract*, where he seeks to creat͘ ͘en-tifies totally with his community, so ͘is dependence on it only as a dep͘ implicitly recognized the f͘ ͘d answer is one of the ma͘ ͘d the *Reveries*, where he create͘ ͘ade for a kind of love that merges th͘ ͘s into a single, psychologically sufficient un͘ ͘s each "better than free." But is this response, like ͘ ͘s proposed by Rousseau, a chimera?

David Gauthier is Emeritus Distinguished Professor of Philosophy at the University of Pittsburgh. He is the author of many articles and several books, most recently *Moral Dealing*, and a Fellow of the Royal Society of Canada.

Rousseau

The Sentiment of Existence

DAVID GAUTHIER

University of Pittsburgh

CAMBRIDGE
UNIVERSITY PRESS

CAMBRIDGE UNIVERSITY PRESS

Cambridge, New York, Melbourne, Madrid, Cape Town, Singapore, São Paulo

Cambridge University Press
40 West 20th Street, New York, NY 10011-4211, USA

www.cambridge.org
Information on this title: www.cambridge.org/9780521809764

First published 2006

Printed in the United States of America

A catalog record for this publication is available from the British Library.

Library of Congress Cataloging in Publication Data

Gauthier, David P.
Rousseau : the sentiment of existence / David Gauthier.
p.   cm.
Includes bibliographical references and index.
ISBN 0-521-80976-2 (hardback : alk. paper) – ISBN 0-521-00759-3
(pbk. : alk. paper)
1. Rousseau, Jean-Jacques, 1712–1778.   2. Social contract.   3. Liberty.   I. Title.
JC179.R88G38   2006
320.1′1 – dc22   2005011550

ISBN-13   978-0-521-80976-4 hardback
ISBN-10   0-521-80976-2 hardback

ISBN-13   978-0-521-00759-7 paperback
ISBN-10   0-521-00759-3 paperback

Contents

Preface

C(ritic): *Another* book on Rousseau? Aren't there more than enough already?

A(uthor): More than enough *bad* books, certainly. I hope I'm not adding to their number.

C: That remains to be seen. I suppose you've convinced yourself you have something new to say about poor Jean-Jacques. But everybody thinks that.

A: Too true. But yes, I do believe you'll find something different here.

C: Rational choice, no doubt. Aren't you the man who reads Prisoner's Dilemmas into every previous moral and political philosopher?

A: Oh, you can find them in Rousseau. But that's not the theme of the book I've written. No graphs. No equations. I'm recording my encounter with Rousseau in the round, bringing the anthropologist, the educator, the political theorist, and the confessionalist together in one extended conversation.

C: And what do these people have to say to each other – and to you?

A: Quite a bit, really. For they are all talking about freedom. The anthropologist recounts the story of its loss – the fall of humankind, we might say. The educator and the political scientist have ideas about its recovery – about redemption.

They don't agree, and they don't convince me – or as I try to show, Rousseau either.

C: And the confessionalist?

A: His effort at redemption is a more complex story. You'll just have to read the book.

C: Must I? Much of this sounds quite commonplace. Fall and redemption narratives are a dime a dozen. You sure this is new stuff?

A: Who knows? I'm not a scholar – as you've reminded me, I'm the Prisoner's Dilemma man. This book records my encounter with Jean-Jacques. Maybe others have had very similar encounters, but I haven't run across them. A very particular interplay between the confessionalist and the social theorist lies at the core of my encounter, and I haven't found that interplay discussed in those parts of the literature I know. But you've mentioned the almost endless number of books on Rousseau – to say nothing of the articles, monographs, dissertations, and so forth. Maybe my ideas are all there somewhere – though I flatter my own acumen if I say that if my ideas were already in the literature, they would have found a more visible place.

C: Which is to say that you believe your book original and consider it important.

A: Original? I hope so. Important? Not many books are really important. I'll be satisfied if there are other persons whose encounters with Rousseau are enhanced by reading mine.

C: Speaking of reading this book, whom do you have in mind?

A: Most people who encounter Rousseau do so in a very limited way. They take a course in philosophy or social thought and read the *Discourse on the Origin of Inequality* and the *Social Contract*. Or they study educational theories and read *Emile*. Or they are interested in French literary masterworks and read the *Confessions* and maybe the *Reveries*. This book offers them a reading of most of the works Rousseau published (and some that he never quite finished) that shows how they are all related. So someone who has read, say, the *Confessions* might read this book to find out how it may fit into the whole of Rousseau's writings.

C: So you've written an introduction to Rousseau's thought?

A: Not in the usual sense. An introduction tries to convey the main ideas of each of Rousseau's works.[1] I try to show how Rousseau develops ideas that link all of them. I don't examine, say, his political theory as such, but I look at how it bears on his concern with freedom, its loss and possible recovery, and with the ideas that Rousseau relates to freedom – slavery, illusion and prestige, help and love.

C: Help and love?

A: Yes – you have to read widely in Rousseau to understand how these ideas are related, and how they inform his account of freedom and its loss. In exploring these connections, this book enables the reader to discover how ideas she finds in one of Rousseau's works are part of a significant larger whole – one that embraces his view of his life as well as his thought.

C: His life. Are you writing a biography of Rousseau focused on his thought?

A: By no means. To be sure, I'm concerned with the life Rousseau constructs for himself in the *Confessions* and the *Reveries*. This life includes his final attempt to show the attainment of redemption, or the recovery of freedom. But his real life, insofar as one can speak of such a thing, falls quite outside my purview.[2]

---

[1] The (Anglophone) reader seeking a very brief introduction to Rousseau's thought might choose Robert Wokler, *Rousseau* (Oxford and New York: Oxford University Press, 1995). If she seeks a fuller but still readily manageable account, she might prefer Timothy O'Hagan, *Rousseau* (London and New York: Routledge, 1999).

[2] Here Maurice Cranston's regrettably unfinished three-volume work may be recommended: *Jean-Jacques: The Early Life and Works of Jean-Jacques Rousseau, 1712–1754* (London: Allen Lane, 1983); *The Noble Savage: Jean-Jacques*

C: You spoke earlier of the bad books on Rousseau –

A: Yes, but I won't talk about them or even name them.

C: What I actually wanted to know is – are there some good ones – other than the introductions and biographies mentioned in your asides?

A: Works that I would recommend to the reader, supplementing my own approach to Rousseau? A very short list, for the Anglophone reader, would have to include *Men and Citizens* by Judith Shklar and *Transparency and Obstruction* by Jean Starobinski. Nicholas Dent has a useful dictionary of Rousseau.[3] Of course there are other good books, but I'm not in the business of assessing them – my interest is in the encounter with Rousseau that I've tried to record.

C: Which brings me to another matter – how did you come to encounter Rousseau? Not your usual line of business, after all.

A: Ah, the powers of chance! My first teaching assignment – in 1958 – was a course in the history of modern political and moral philosophy – "modern" being used to cover the period from 1600 to 1900. I began with the social contract figures. Hobbes was the first person to catch my philosophical attention – largely because Howard Warrender showed that the tools of modern analytic philosophy could be used to illuminate his thought.[4]

Rousseau, 1754–1762 (London: Allen Lane, 1991); and *The Solitary Self: Jean-Jacques Rousseau in Exile and Adversity* (London: Allen Lane, 1997), with a foreword by Sanford Lakoff. Also to be recommended: Jean Guéhenno, *Jean-Jacques Rousseau*, vol. 1, 1712–1758; vol. 2, 1758–1778, English translation by J. and D. Weightman (London: Routledge and Kegan Paul, 1966).

[3] See Judith Shklar, *Men and Citizens: A Study of Rousseau's Social Theory* (Cambridge: Cambridge University Press, 1969); Jean Starobinski, *Jean-Jacques Rousseau: Transparency and Obstruction*, English translation by Arthur Goldhammer (Chicago and London: University of Chicago Press, 1988); and N. J. H. Dent, *A Rousseau Dictionary* (Oxford: Blackwell, 1992).

[4] See Howard Warrender, *The Political Philosophy of Hobbes: His Theory of Obligation* (Oxford: Clarendon Press, 1957). Warrender is, I have argued, mistaken in his

C: You could hardly have found a parallel in that regard with Rousseau.

A: Quite right. Rousseau first appealed to my political self, because of the communitarian ideal of *Political Economy* and the *Social Contract*. In those far off days I found myself on the fringe of the cultural socialism that made the British new left so exciting. Rousseau seemed to fit into all that.

C: But that hardly explains your present book. You're no longer a leftist.

A: Heavens, no. I learned some economics and abandoned communitarian socialism for individualistic liberalism.

C: And Jean-Jacques?

A: Well, first of all I found him critiquing, at least implicitly, his apparent communitarianism – and that is present in my book. But that's not the deepest point.

C: Go on.

A: Whatever one makes of the idea that contemporary Western society alienates the individual from his true nature, Rousseau was the first, I think, to express it, and to seek a way to restore man to himself. (Restoring woman to herself is another matter, rather neglected by Rousseau.) Exploring this aspect of Rousseau's thought launched me on my present inquiry, although the tale came to prove more complex than I had expected and to possess a quite unexpected new dimension when Rousseau's *maman*, Madame de Warens, and his novelistic heroine, Julie, joined the account. For their role is to suggest that man can be restored to himself only by finding a soul mate – another idea that Rousseau pioneers.

---

reading of Hobbes, which in any case has no direct bearing on Rousseau, but had I not read Warrender, I might never have taken an interest in the history of political philosophy.

C: I think we're beginning to trespass on the text. So one final
   question. You've recorded an encounter with Rousseau. Is
   he really worth the encounter?

A: Some final question! Of course there are people who would
   want to dismiss him as a paranoid narcissist. Others, though,
   might insist that we need a paranoid narcissist to reveal the
   dark beauty of our world.

A NOTE ON TRANSLATING ROUSSEAU

To convey the nature of my encounter with Rousseau, I must let
him speak for himself much of the time. But this is a book written
in English and primarily for Anglophone readers. So Rousseau
must speak in translation.[5] Whose?

Most of Rousseau's writings are now available in the set of
Collected Writings with Roger D. Masters and Christopher Kelly as
series editors.[6] These translations are of fine quality and employ
a consistent terminology. Using them enables the reader who
wishes to place a quoted passage in its context to do so readily
and without any terminological confusion. So I have chosen –
most of the time – to use them.[7]

But in some passages Rousseau speaks to me differently than
he did to the translators in this series. When he does, I have
allowed myself to alter their translations – though I have used
footnotes to alert the reader to the alteration.

---

[5] For readers who want to refer to the French original, I give references in
the text to the *Oeuvres complètes*, series editors Bernard Gagnebin and Marcel
Raymond (Paris: Gallimard, Bibliothèque de la Pléiade, 5 vols., 1959–95). I
use the abbreviation OC followed by the volume and page numbers. I also give
references to OC when I am not using a translation of Rousseau's text but only
alluding to it.

[6] The series is published for Dartmouth University by the University Press of New
England (Hanover, NH, and London: 10 vols. to date, 1990–2004).

[7] Passages quoted from volumes in this series are identified by CW, followed by
the volume and page numbers.

And in one work – Rousseau's *Pygmalion* – I have simply preferred my own translations, which I think provide a better fit to my reading of the text.

Then there are those writings not yet translated (as of late 2004) in the *Collected Writings. Emile* provides no problem – there is a splendid translation by Allan Bloom,[8] though even here I have allowed myself the odd alteration. *Considerations on the Government of Poland* has been translated by Victor Gourevitch[9] – indeed, a case could be made for using his translations of Rousseau's other political writings. But I judged that the *Collected Writings* would become the standard English reference.

There are three other works of Rousseau that I have quoted but that have not been translated into English so far as I know. These are the *Epistle to Parisot, Emile and Sophie,* and *Queen Whimsy* (*La Reine fantasque*). The translations are therefore my own.

A NOTE ON HOW THIS BOOK CAME TO BE

In 1992, I delivered a set of lectures, "Three Walks with a Solitary: Rediscovering Rousseau," as Cecil H. and Ida Green Visiting Professor at the University of British Columbia. And in 1996, I delivered another set of three lectures, "Jean-Jacques's Last Promenade," as F. E. L. Priestley Memorial Lecturer at the University of Toronto. These lectures were drafted while I held a Visiting Fellowship in the Research School of Social Sciences at the Australian National University.

I then integrated and expanded both sets of lectures into a single set of six, "The Social and the Solitary," delivered in 1998

---

[8] See Allan Bloom (ed. and tr.), *Emile, or On Education* (New York: Basic Books, 1979). Passages quoted are identified in the text by Bl followed by the page number.

[9] See Victor Gourevitch (ed. and tr.), *Rousseau: The Social Contract and Other Later Political Writings* (Cambridge: Cambridge University Press, 1997). Passages quoted are identified in the text by Go followed by the page number.

as Benedict Lecturer in the History of Political Philosophy at Boston University, in conjunction with a graduate seminar on Rousseau offered by Knud Haakonssen. These lectures formed the first draft of the present book.

I wrote the second draft in 2000 on a sabbatical leave from the University of Pittsburgh spent happily in Paris, where I presented versions of Chapters 4 and 5 (in English!) to a seminar conducted by Monique Canto-Sperber at the Centre de Recherche en Épistémologie Appliquée (CREA) of the École Polytechnique.

It has taken me a ridiculously long time to complete a final draft.

I am indebted to many persons for comments, questions, and discussion at the academic institutions just mentioned, and at several other universities where I have presented papers on Rousseau. My encounters with these persons have enhanced the encounter with Rousseau related in this book.

Rousseau

The Sentiment of Existence

1

Legends of the Fall

His last writings are the *Reveries of the Solitary Walker.* Each reverie
is identified as a promenade, so that, he tells us, they are "a
faithful record of my solitary walks and of the reveries which fill
them." (CW8.9, OC1.1002) They are the walks of a man "alone
on earth" (CW8.3, OC1.995), in which, as he says, "I will apply
the barometer to my soul." (CW8.7, OC1.1000–1) The last – the
tenth – is unfinished, a walk from which he does not return. In
the five volumes of his collected works, it occupies two pages.
And yet I exaggerate only slightly in saying that my aim in this
book – in this journey that I invite you to take with Jean-Jacques
Rousseau – is to understand that final promenade, why it says
what it says, why it does not say what it does not say. To reach that
walk will be my end, as it was his end. It is fitting that we should
begin by joining Rousseau on another walk.

He is in Paris, a man of thirty-seven with literary and musical aspirations as yet unfulfilled, an associate of the intellectuals
whom we have come to know as the *philosophes.* He is a collabora-
tor with Denis Diderot, who had embarked on the great project
of his life, the *Encyclopedia* that was to synthesize the knowledge
and outlook of the Enlightenment. Diderot's skeptical writings
having led to his brief and quite comfortable imprisonment in
the chateau of Vincennes, Rousseau undertook frequent walks
from Paris to visit his friend. I shall let Rousseau tell the story.

That year 1749 the Summer was excessively hot. From Paris to Vincennes adds up to two leagues. . . . The trees on the road, always pruned in the fashion of the country, gave almost no shade; and often exhausted from the heat and fatigue, I spread out on the ground when I was not able to go any farther. I took it into my head to take some book along to moderate my pace. One day I took the *Mercury of France* and while walking and glancing over it I fell upon this question proposed by the Academy of Dijon for the prize for the following year: *Has the progress of the sciences and arts tended to corrupt or purify morals?*

  At the moment of that reading I saw another universe and I became another man. (CW5.294, OC1.350–1)

Thus the account in his autobiography, the *Confessions*. In his *Second Letter to M. de Malesherbes*, Rousseau continues,

I let myself fall under one of the trees of the avenue, and I pass a half-hour there in such an agitation that when I got up again I noticed the whole front of my coat soaked with my tears without having felt that I shed them. Oh Sir, if I had ever been able to write a quarter of what I saw and felt under that tree, how clearly I would have made all the contradictions of the social system seen, with what strength I would have exposed all the abuses of our institutions, with what simplicity I would have demonstrated that man is naturally good and that it is from these institutions alone that men become wicked. Everything that I was able to retain of these crowds of great truths which illuminated me under that tree in a quarter of an hour has been weakly scattered about in my three principal writings. (CW5.575, OC1.1135–6)

The first of the three works to which Rousseau refers is the *Discourse on the Sciences and Arts*, in which he responds to the question that triggered his illumination – whether the progress of the arts and sciences has corrupted or purified morals – and which, winning the prize of the Academy of Dijon, brought him instant notoriety. The second is the *Discourse on the Origin of Inequality*, his great work of philosophical anthropology that is the main concern of this first chapter. And the third is the *Emile*, Rousseau's study of the education of the individual, which will provide the themes for the second chapter.

"Has the restoration of the Sciences and Arts tended to purify or corrupt Morals?" (CW2.4, OC3.5) "Corrupt" is Rousseau's addition. The Academy of Dijon asked whether the restoration of the sciences and arts had tended to purify morals. In the first sentence of his *Discourse* Rousseau rephrased the question as a choice between alternatives: purification or corruption? In his account in the *Confessions* (quoted earlier), Rousseau amended the question yet again in reordering the alternatives: to corrupt or to purify morals. The idea of corruption, at most implicit in the Academy's question, becomes Rousseau's guiding thread. Faced with the issue, his response was immediate: the moral qualities thrive in simplicity, both material and mental, but the arts and sciences bring complexity, luxury, and with luxury, dissoluteness. In the *Discourse on the Sciences and Arts*, Rousseau focuses on the habits of life that accompany learning and culture, the decline of the martial virtues, the increase in material needs. But his deeper concern is with the changes that occur in human beings as they develop the capacities needed for the progress of the sciences and arts – as they become reasoning and reflective beings. And this concern brings us to the *Discourse on the Origin of Inequality*. Addressing his fellow men, Rousseau proclaims: "O Man . . . here is your history as I believed to read it[1] . . . in Nature, which never lies. Everything that comes from Nature will be true; there will be nothing false except what I have involuntarily put in of my own." (CW3.19, OC3.133) And what he reads is the beginning of humankind in solitude, and the gradual emergence of society; our history is that of a solitary creature becoming social. It is this progression that Rousseau identifies as corruption.

We shall sit with Rousseau under the tree on the way to Vincennes, and learn our history. But before we do so, I want to insert a further word of anticipation. I have mentioned the *Reveries*, his last writings, where he begins with the words "I am

---

[1] Bush et al. translation, "it to read"; French "*la lire.*"

now alone on earth. . . . [I] the most sociable and the most loving of humans." (CW8.3, OC1.995) He is the social creature become once more solitary, writing "my reveries only for myself" (CW8.8, OC1.1001) and asking, "But I, detached from them [all other men] and from everything, what am I myself?" (CW8.3, OC1.995)[2] From reading the history of humankind in nature to applying the barometer to his soul, from learning how humans became social to finding himself become solitary – this is the journey we are about to take with Rousseau.

Why take this journey? One answer would be that Rousseau, whether telling us of our history or of his own condition, whether examining the social contract or writing his confessions, illuminates one of the deep and enduring themes that troubles both our social thought and our social practice – the relationship between individual and community. But for the most part I shall let that illumination emerge implicitly. Another answer appears in my title for this first chapter, "Legends of the Fall." The history Rousseau recounts is more than a story of social transformation, and with it the development of reason and reflection. Above all it is a moral history, of loss of innocence and descent into corruption. It expresses, almost for the first time, the angst that has become familiar to us who inhabit the modern world – a sense of isolation from others and alienation from society coupled with nostalgia for a past perhaps remembered, perhaps imagined. And this moral history poses for Rousseau the problem that informs all of his further writings – can paradise be regained? He will look for the redemption of human beings, in the education of the individual, collectively in politics and in the education of the citizen, and – finally – personally, in his own experience, and in love.

But enough of anticipation. Let us now begin at the beginning – with our earliest human ancestors, as Rousseau depicts

[2] "myself" added to Butterworth tr.; Fr. "*que suis-je moi-même?*".

them. Each had an instinctive concern for self-preservation, the most primitive form of what Rousseau calls *amour de soi*, but this gave rise only to very simple desires and needs – for food and drink, for shelter from inclement weather, intermittently for sex. And each was naturally self-sufficient, able to provide for his few needs through his own efforts. Rousseau postulates no *social* desires or interests, nothing that would bring human beings together except in the brief coupling of sexual intercourse. To be sure, from this coupling the female found herself from time to time with a child, but our ancestors were more robust, matured physically more quickly, and underwent a much simpler and briefer mental development. To satisfy their needs, the first humans required little memory, even less foresight, and only a limited awareness of their environment. And given their small numbers and the abundance of the earth's provisions, their reasoning was as limited as their awareness. Their simple ends were readily secured without any complex calculation of means.

Although they lacked sociability, their instinctive concern with preservation was moderated by "a natural repugnance to see any sensitive Being perish or suffer, principally those like ourselves." (CW3.15, OC3.126) This repugnance, which Rousseau calls pity or commiseration, varies in strength with the extent of identification with the sufferer. Before human beings learned to reason, this identification was direct, but when reason develops, it "turns man back upon himself, . . . [and] separates him from all that bothers and afflicts him." (CW3.37, OC3.156)

A concern with one's preservation, and a repugnance for suffering, do not in themselves distinguish human beings from other animals, which, following the Cartesian view, Rousseau represents as self-sustaining mechanisms. He represents human beings also as such mechanisms, but distinguishes them from other animals as possessing two unique characteristics – free will, and "la faculté de se perfectionner" (OC3.142), the faculty of self-perfection, or perfectibility. Free will is no doubt presupposed

by but plays little active part in Rousseau's argument, but perfectibility is central; indeed, without perfectibility there would be
no moral history of humankind for Rousseau to recount. As he
insists, it is the "faculty which, with the aid of circumstances, successively develops all the others, and resides among us as much
in the species as in the individual. By contrast an animal is at
the end of a few months what it will be all its life; and its species
is at the end of a thousand years what it was the first year of
that thousand." (CW3.26, OC3.142) Perfectibility, and its moral
consequences, thus apply to both the individual person and the
human species. And as we shall see, the moral consequences tend
to be negative. Indeed, the price human beings pay for their perfectibility is shown in Rousseau's famous remark at the beginning
of the *Social Contract*, that "Man was/is born free, and everywhere
he is in chains." (CW4.131, OC3.351) For in Rousseau's account
of the history of the human race, in perfecting itself humankind
loses its natural liberty, so that the species, which once consisted
of free individuals, is now made up of slaves, and each contemporary human being, who is himself or herself born to be free,
comes to share his fellows' chains.

But we have yet to review our history. Perfectibility was only
latent in our earliest ancestors. They lived in what Rousseau
describes as the condition of natural liberty. Liberty here has
nothing to do with the free will that Rousseau ascribes to humans,
but rather with the adequacy of each person's powers to meet his
or her needs and desires. In *Emile*, he writes, "Your freedom and
your power extend only as far as your natural strength, and not
beyond. All the rest is only slavery, illusion and prestige.[3] . . .
The truly free man wants only what he can do and does what he
pleases. That is my fundamental maxim." (Bl.83–4, OC4.308–
9) Our ancestors thus were free, but unaware of their freedom,
since they had not developed the capacity to reflect on their

[3] Bloom tr., "deception."

condition. Nothing drove them to reflect, and humans, like all animals, are naturally lazy, doing no more than their needs and desires require. Perfectibility remains latent so long as natural powers suffice to meet equally natural needs.

Rousseau contrasts the liberty that lies in the harmony of power and desire with three alternative conditions: slavery, illusion, and prestige. Each of these is a way of being unfree, a way in which one's powers fail to be adequate to meet one's needs. In tracing the course of human development, we should be able to understand how slavery and prestige come to replace natural liberty. But what of illusion? We might intuitively suppose that it renders a person unfree by depriving him of a true awareness, whether of his powers, his needs and desires, or his circumstances. But as our journey continues, in later chapters we shall find that the role of illusion is in fact much deeper, and its relation to liberty less straightforward, than a simple contrast would imply.

Before concluding this retrospective look at human origins, we need to note what may at first seem but one further detail. Rousseau says, "Man's first sentiment was that of his existence, his first care that of his preservation." (CW3.43, OC3.164) Preservation has figured centrally in his account of human and indeed of animal nature; one might easily overlook reference to a sentiment about which at first nothing more is asserted than its original presence. But the sentiment of existence is at the core of Rousseau's understanding of his fellows and of himself; the individual is revealed in how he senses his existence. Indeed, we might say – although this is to interpret and not to quote Rousseau – that perfectibility manifests itself in the unfolding of the sentiment of existence.

Rousseau has described our Eden, but it is an unconscious Eden, its inhabitants free, but with no awareness of their freedom, happy, but only in not knowing their misery (v. OC3.283), "stupid [and] limited." (CW4.141, OC3.364) He tells us little about how our ancestors came to leave it – population increased gradually, and so resources once abundant became scarce; humankind spread over the face of the earth, and so some came to inhabit less clement regions. These changes have no direct effect on needs and desires; rather, they affect the adequacy of human powers to meet those desires. Greater awareness of circumstances, increased memory and foresight, more sophisticated instrumental reasoning, all became necessary to survive in straitened circumstances. Other animals would perish, unable to adapt, but perfectibility manifests itself in newly realized mental capacities.

And now we begin to approach the fundamental ambiguity at the heart of human perfectibility – the ambiguity that Rousseau recognized in denying that our progress in culture and knowledge brings moral progress in its train. Perfectibility first affects our cognitive capacities. But its effects extend further, to our affective capacities, and also to our moral capacities. Let us take these in turn. Perfectibility expands our awareness, but this expanded awareness reveals new objects, not only to our intellect, but also to our appetites. It expands our deliberations, but these expanded deliberations reveal not only new ways of satisfying existing appetites, but also new ways of directing and developing those appetites. Our appetitive capacities, just as our mental capacities, are perfectible; their scope is not limited to its original extent. And so we find ourselves, not only with new understandings, but also with new prospects and new concerns.

In seeking better ways of satisfying existing needs and desires, we find also new desires and passions that demand satisfaction. And so human beings find themselves on a treadmill; each step that they take toward restoring the balance between their powers and their desires leads them to new desires and passions that dislocate the balance. Once human beings sense themselves as unfree, in the grip of desires that they cannot satisfy, then their attempts to free themselves, even if successful in terms of their original concerns, put them in the grip of yet further desires. If we think of human history as beginning with the first imbalance between powers and needs that deprived human beings of their original liberty, we must ask if the further course of human history reveals some point at which the balance is restored, and with it liberty, or reveals instead a progressively increasing imbalance that drives human beings further and further from the prospect of freedom.

But the course of human history is not simply an interplay, however complex, of an increasingly perfected understanding and an increasingly expanded appetite. As human beings become aware of their surroundings, they also become aware of their fellows. Leaving aside that aspect which is relevant only to sexual gratification, Rousseau relates awareness of one's fellows to a twofold concern. On the one hand, there are those occasions, originally rare, in which common interest invites each to seek and rely on the assistance of others. On the other hand, there are those occasions, originally rarer, in which competitive interest leads each to suspect and endeavor to overcome others. Both cooperative and competitive interests invite individuals to make comparisons between themselves and others – to recognize those respects in which each is or may be useful to his or her fellows, and those in which each is or may be harmful. And in these comparisons we find the origin of our moral sensibilities.

Rousseau represents this as the conversion of *amour de soi* into *amour propre*. *Amour de soi(-même)* is no more than the care each person – indeed, each animal – has for its own preservation. It is a love centered on the self and addressed to its natural needs; it involves no awareness of others, much less comparison between self and others. But as awareness of others develops, this self-love is transformed into *amour propre*, a love centered on the relation between the self and others and addressed to comparative advantage. As Rousseau treats it in the *Discourse on the Origin of Inequality*, it is a "relative sentiment, artificial and born in

Society, which inclines each individual to have a greater esteem for himself than for anyone else." (CW3.91, OC3.219) In his first mention of it, he claims that *amour propre* "inspires in men all the harm they do to one another" (ibid.), but as we shall find, its moral status proves more complex than this purely negative judgment would suggest. The extensions and transformations of *amour propre* lie at the heart of Rousseau's redemptive quest.

Amour de soi is linked to our sentiment of existence. As long as it alone holds sway, each person unreflectively senses his existence in himself. But as it comes to be transformed into *amour propre*, each senses his existence not in himself, but in his relation to those whom he perceives as other. It is the regard that others have for me, their concern with my power, or their contempt for my lack of power, their valuing or disdaining my assistance, their fearing or ignoring my opposition, that form the basis of my own self-conception. I am no longer psychologically self-sufficient, and so no longer free; I seek the recognition of the other that confers prestige. But this loss of freedom depends on distinguishing self and other, and Rousseau does not suppose that the earliest social relationships rested on this distinction.

In the early stages of human history, the need to cooperate in order to satisfy increasingly expansive desires under increasingly adverse circumstances led to the formation of small groups, based on family relationships. Rousseau believes that these groups brought stability to human affairs, that each group was able to establish self-sufficiency without coming into frequent conflict with its neighbors. Within the horizon set by the group, the balance between powers and needs was restored; each could expect the resources of the group to be available to meet his needs and desires, and each could recognize those resources as generally sufficient. Thus although each individual was materially dependent on the fellow members of his family group, Rousseau supposes that psychologically each individual did not experience his condition as one of dependence, and so of lack of liberty, because he identified himself with his family, and regarded the powers of the group as his own powers, available to meet his needs.

It might be thought that the more completely an individual identifies himself with his family, the more he senses his existence in relation to persons other than himself. This would make the family the primary locus of *amour propre*, of the desire to be foremost, and of unfreedom. But this is not Rousseau's view. In identifying with his family, an individual senses himself as part of a single entity of which his kin are also a part, and so he does not relate himself to them as "other." The primary manifestation of *amour propre*, at this stage of human and social development, was to be found not within the family, but in the festivals that brought members of different families, and especially the young, together to sing and dance. "The one who sang or danced the best, the handsomest, the strongest, the most adroit, or the most eloquent became the most highly considered; and that was the first step toward inequality and, at the same time, toward vice." (CW3.47, OC3.169–70) In the *Essay on the Origin of Languages*,[4] Rousseau envisages these festivals as occurring around the wells where the young from different families were sent to fetch water. Smitten with their new acquaintances, they found that "[i]mperceptibly water became more necessary, the livestock were thirsty more often; they arrived in haste and parted reluctantly. . . . There the first festivals took place." (CW7.314, OC5.406) And in those festivals, expressive gestures were no longer sufficient for communication; not only *amour propre*, but speech was born. And they were indeed born together, for the first words, Rousseau tells us, were *aimez-moi* – "love me." (CW7.316, OC5.408) In speech, then, each relates himself to his fellows, seeking from them the deepest form of recognition – love.

---

4 This work remained unpublished in Rousseau's lifetime.

Amour propre may be the sentiment that "inspires men with all the evils they do one another," but it is also inextricably tied to love. And love, as we shall find when we have accompanied Rousseau to his final promenade, is at the center of his last redemptive vision. Here, however, our interest is not in the final significance of humankind's first words, but in their origin – the origin of language, which clearly fascinated Rousseau, as it did many of his contemporaries. He understands language as a social phenomenon, emerging in the same circumstances that brought human beings into society; indeed, in the *Discourse on the Origin of Inequality* he treats the origins of language and society as a chicken-and-egg problem. But in the *Essay on the Origin of Languages*, Rousseau insists that gestures were sufficient for the first social groupings – families. In a footnote, he insists that "[g]enuine languages do not at all have a domestic origin. . . . The Savages of America almost never speak except outside of their homes; each keeps silent in his cabin, he speaks[5] to his family by signs." (CW7.305n., OC5.395n.) Only when members of different families came into contact did speech manifest itself, and it took two fundamentally different forms. Rousseau distinguishes southern and northern languages; it is the former that arose in festivals around the wells and that began in the expression of each person's primary desire when faced with his fellows: "Love me!" But there is little love in a cold climate; the northern languages arose out of need rather than passion, and began in the expression of each person's primary need when faced with his fellows: "Help me!" (v. CW7.316, OC5.408) In the French, the first words are of course *aimez-moi* and *aidez-moi*; their similarity is not accidental. Although both the cry for love and the demand for help are expressive of *amour propre*, we shall find that they work contrary effects on our moral sensibilities. In the *Discourse on the Origin of Inequality*, Rousseau is primarily concerned with

[5] Scott tr., "spoke"; Fr. "*parle*."

the effects of the demand for help. Recounting these, we learn the legends of the Fall.

The negative effects of *amour propre* have yet to become fully manifest. Perfectibility has begun to emerge from latency with the enlargement of both our understanding and our appetite, the appearance of the family as the first form of society and, in the first festivals, the emergence of human relationships based on comparison. But it has yet to give rise to any deep form of dependence among human beings. It is time to move on, to end our look at what Rousseau judges the happiest and longest-lasting epoch in the development of human faculties. We must ask how our ancestors came to leave this second Eden, this paradise of the family.

"For the Poet it is gold and silver, but for the Philosopher it is iron and wheat which have Civilized men and ruined the human Race." (CW3.49, OC3.171) Metallurgy and agriculture are the arts that corrupted and denatured us. Their discovery brought to an end the self-sufficiency of the family; for the first time, it became advantageous and even unavoidable to specialize in but one of the necessities of life. Rousseau does not deny that these arts brought new material wealth to humankind. But he notes the price of this wealth – that each became dependent on another, on someone with a different way of life, a different and indeed opposed goal. Each came to speak the fatal words, *aidez-moi*, but to another person who did not share his interests. The farmer and the metalworker must trade to live, and the more advantageous the terms of trade for the farmer, the less advantageous they are for the metalworker. To be sure, each may be materially better off than in the era of familial society, but we must distinguish between commodities, which are in increased and perhaps ever-increasing supply, and positional goods, whose supply is fixed – for every gain, there must be a corresponding loss.

In the era of self-sufficient families, each one functioned – at least in Rousseau's vision – as a cooperative whole, and none concerned itself about its neighbors. Each family expressed its own *amour de soi*, in which the sentiment of existence primitively identified with the self, the *moi*, came to be extended to the group, the *nous*. All sensed their existence in the family, and finding the powers of the family adequate to meet their needs, felt themselves free. Not comparing itself with others, the self-sufficient family did not develop *amour propre*. But with the division of labor between cultivators and craftsmen, each family, no longer self-sufficient, began to function as a trading unit in a larger market. Each had to concern itself with its neighbors, and each soon found itself moved both by simple material interest and by *amour propre* to seek to be foremost. Favorable recognition from others contributed to material success in trade, and confirmed the sentiment of existence. And so the positional goods one acquired – one's status or prestige vis-à-vis one's fellows – came to be of central importance. In this way the material dependence inherent in the division of labor and the consequent necessity of trade gave rise to psychological dependence. For Rousseau, as later for Marx, the primary effect of the division of labor is not to enrich persons by giving them access to the capacities and powers of their fellows, or to enhance their lives by enabling them to specialize in those activities for which they have the greatest aptitude, but rather to enslave them by making the exercise of their own capacities dependent on their fellows' alien wills.

The motivational efficacy of positional goods may seem difficult to explain, especially in the light of Rousseau's insistence that human beings, like all other animals, are naturally lazy, exerting themselves no more than they feel necessary. Why should we prove more willing to exert ourselves for positional goods, which exist only in opinion, than for substantial goods, which have a real, material existence? We have already supplied part of the answer – positional goods may arise from opinion, but they bring material benefits. The farmer whose produce is judged best commands the highest price. But for Rousseau the appeal of positional goods goes beyond any material advantages that they may bring, and is inherent in perfectibility. As long as one remains unaware both of the world and of other human beings, except insofar as these relate directly to one's natural needs, one has no measure of oneself that would call perfectibility into full play. But in developing a more extensive awareness of things, one acquires passions that extend beyond natural need, and require the assistance of others for their gratification. And in developing an awareness of persons, of others who are not oneself but are nevertheless like oneself, one comes to possess a measure of how far one surpasses or falls short of those others in one's ability to meet one's needs and gratify one's desires and passions. And this measure reflects one's standing in the eyes of those others on whom one's gratification depends. The capacity to perfect oneself then becomes fully active, and expresses itself in *amour propre*, the drive to be foremost.

Thus in Rousseau's story of human development, hostile competition comes to supplant peaceful cooperation. In the original, pre-social condition of humankind, opportunities for cooperation, although few, outnumbered the circumstances that created competition. In the epoch of familial societies, cooperation within the family was the dominant form of interaction. But in the new epoch initiated by the division of labor, competition became dominant, and *amour propre* took on its virulent form. Rousseau quickly describes the new order – "all our faculties developed, memory and imagination in play, amour propre aroused, reason rendered active, and the mind having almost reached the limit of the perfection of which it is susceptible." (CW3.51, OC3.174) Perfectibility has done its work in enlarging our capacities, but at the full price of its moral effects. Each person sought to be foremost, but to be dependent on one's fellows means that to *be* foremost is to *seem* foremost to them. And so "to be and to appear[6] to be became two altogether different things." (Ibid.) Or perhaps more precisely, whereas previously a person was concerned with *what he is*, with the adequacy of his own powers to meet his needs and desires, he came now to be concerned with *how he appears*, for this determined whether others would use their powers to help meet his needs and desires. Whereas previously a person would appear *as he is*, now he is *as he appears*.

I mentioned earlier the three conditions that Rousseau contrasts with liberty: slavery, illusion, and prestige. The slave fails to gain the recognition of his or her fellows and can survive only by literal abasement, by being a person entirely for another and not for himself. But what of the person who has succeeded in gaining recognition? He survives on prestige, on maintaining the good opinion of others. Whatever real qualities the prestigious person possesses, what matters are only the qualities others ascribe to him. He cannot be free, since the powers requisite to meet his needs and desires are not his own; rather, they are the powers he is believed to possess, for it is these that affect the responses of others, and so determine whether he will gain satisfaction. In a brief passage suggestive of the master-slave dialectic that Hegel will develop, Rousseau notes that "having formerly been free and independent, behold man, due to a multitude of new needs, subjected so to speak . . . especially to his fellows, whose slave he becomes in a sense even in becoming their master; rich, he needs their services; poor, he needs their help." (CW3.51– 2, OC3.174–5) The master's condition is one of psychological slavery.

The person who gains prestige is viewed by others as a source of assistance, and so gains their help in return. But more – he is viewed by others as willing to assist them. Each wants to be viewed in this way, to appear as a friend, as someone who willingly

---

[6] Bush tr., "seem."

seeks the good of his fellows. But what each really wants is for others to seek his good. Friendship is feigned; Rousseau saw the persons of his time as masked, friendly false faces concealing their real hostility. A person concerned with how he is, with how his powers relate to his needs, is concerned with reality. But a person concerned with how he appears, wanting to use others by seeming their friend, is concerned with illusion.

The new order – or disorder – is a condition of war. Indeed, although Rousseau does not acknowledge it, it is the same war of every man against every man that Thomas Hobbes, a century earlier, had claimed to be our natural or original condition. For Rousseau, of course, it is the *un*natural, *un*original condition that results from the unrestrained operation of human perfectibility. But whereas in Hobbes's thought it is the final horror from which only an absolutist political order can rescue us, for Rousseau it is but one stage in the long Fall of humankind. The worst is yet to come.

The division of labor initiates society. But the dynamic of the descent into slavery begins when this division is underpinned by the right of property. Rousseau opens the second part of the *Discourse on the Origin of Inequality* with this ringing declaration:

The first person who, having fenced off a plot of ground, took it into his head to say *this is mine* and found people simple enough to believe him, was the true founder of civil society. What crimes, wars, murders, what miseries and horrors would the human Race have been spared by someone who, uprooting the stakes or filling in the ditch, had shouted to his fellows: Beware of listening to this impostor; you are lost if you forget that the fruits belong to all and the Earth to no one! (CW3.43, OC3.164)

The division of labor is sustained by a division over the control of resources and products. Land is in the hands of the farmers, iron and the means to work it in the hands of the metalworkers. But control is a power, not a right; de facto possession is not de jure property. The discoveries of agriculture and metalworking in themselves bring no rights to those who practice these arts. Men made claims to land or to tools based on occupancy, possession, and production – claims that might at first have been generally honored but came increasingly to be ignored in the growing disorder. Rousseau supposes that those with most to lose, those whose possessions and productivity were greatest, recognized more clearly than their fellows both the general need for order, and the particular advantage to themselves of basing this order on the status quo, converting de facto possession into de jure property. For in fixing property rights, the difference between rich and poor was also fixed; ephemeral inequalities in wealth, subject to being overthrown by a thousand circumstances, became permanent.

Property rights provide the dynamic force in the history of humankind. Rousseau identifies three stages, involving progressively increasing inequality and alienation.

[T]he establishment of the Law and of the Right of property was the first stage, the institution of the Magistracy the second, and the third and last was the changing of legitimate power into arbitrary power. So that the status of rich and poor was authorized by the first Epoch, that of powerful and weak by the second, and by the third that of Master and Slave, which is the last degree of inequality. (CW3.62, OC3.187)

Property was introduced to overcome the insecurity of mere possession, but property rights needed enforcement. And so magistracy was instituted to uphold the right of property. De facto power was converted into de jure authority. But when the poor and weak finally realized that they were the losers in this new world ruled by *amour propre*, they came to stake all on a violent attempt, not so much to undo the new order, but to seize for themselves the seats of the wealthy and powerful. Since they had not escaped the grip of *amour propre*, they sought to be themselves foremost. Whether their insurrection succeeded or was suppressed, the result was the same – the conversion of magistracy into arbitrary command, in which rulers emerged as masters, and subjects as slaves. The rights of property and magistracy became the means of domination and repression.

And so, sitting under the tree with Rousseau for a quarter of an hour – or indeed, since our minds are not elevated with such a sublime rush of ideas, a little longer so that we might begin to digest his thoughts – we have learned our history. He is now impatient to be on his way to Vincennes, where he will show Diderot the notice from the Academy of Dijon, and be encouraged to compete for the prize that he will win. But before we let him leave us, so that we may spend a few moments on our own reflecting on what he has been saying, we need to bring together the beginning and the end – the original human being as nature made him, – or perhaps her, and the modern human being as society made him. Although Rousseau of course uses the male pronoun throughout, it would not be inappropriate to think of our original human being as female, since despite Rousseau's own preoccupations that led him to hold that "the only goods he knows in the Universe are nourishment, a female, and repose" (CW3.27, OC3.143), it is clear that it is the mothers rather than the fathers who ensure the continuation of the species in its original condition. But it is the men, holding wealth and power, who determine the alienated and denatured conditions under which human beings exist in society, and so we may appropriately think of Rousseau's modern human being as male.

The savage "breathes only repose and freedom; he wants only to live and remain idle"; the citizen "torments himself incessantly in order to seek still more laborious occupations." (CW3.66, OC3.192) In order for the savage

to see the good of so many cares, the words *power* and *reputation* would have to have a meaning in his mind; he would have to learn that there is a kind of men who count for something the consideration of the rest of the universe and who know how to be happy and content with themselves on the testimony of others rather than on their own. Such is, in fact, the genuine cause of all these differences: the Savage lives within himself; the sociable man, always outside of himself, knows how to live only in the opinion of others; and it is, so to speak, from their judgment alone that he draws the sentiment of his own existence. (CW3.66, OC3.193)

The reality of the self is only its appearance in the other.

Our first, primary sentiment is that of our existence. A human being, as nature has made him, finds that sentiment within himself. By himself, he is "a perfect and solitary whole" (CW4.155, OC3.381), to use words that we shall encounter again. Being dependent on nothing beyond for his sense of self, he is in the deepest sense a free being. But his perfection – the perfection of solitude – is lost as humanity undergoes the process of perfectibility. As we become reasoning animals, our sense of self undergoes profound modifications. As the self is distinguished from the other, the sense of one's own existence becomes more intense, more focused. Finding no obstacles to his preservation, the natural human being lives in a state of repose; his sense of self needs no expression. But as *amour propre* emerges from the growing awareness of the relations between self and other, the sense of self enters into our first words – "Love me!" "Help me!" The self now must assert itself in its cry for love or demand for help.

Understanding the demand for love, and its implications for the sense of one's existence, is a task for later chapters. Here I have been exploring Rousseau's account of the demand for help, and its implications. In speaking the words *aidez-moi*, each person seeks access to powers adequate to meet his needs. He seeks freedom. He aims at strengthening himself. But the powers he seeks depend on the wills of others, which are directed to their needs, not his. Even if he succeeds in gaining access to their powers, he makes himself dependent on them, and so in a deeper sense enslaves and weakens himself. His demand for help is directed outside, to the other who must validate his sense of self by extending the demanded help. The *moi* survives only in its conjunction with *aidez*. It is from the other's judgment, from his response to the demand, that the social or, we might say, socialized individual takes the sentiment of his existence. In himself, he is nothing; where the savage finds his[7] sentiment of existence, the socialized individual would find only emptiness. And so, being totally dependent on what is alien to himself – on what he can encounter only as the object of his demand – for the very sentiment of his own existence, he is in the deepest sense unfree. And if he is deprived of help, then he loses the only human status left for him – he has no *prestige*. Empty of all reality in himself, existing only in his appearance for the alien others, lacking a nature of his own, he has fallen into nothingness.

We have followed Rousseau's account of human perfectibility through to what we might call, anachronistically, the dialectic of slavery and prestige. We have traced his history of humankind, from solitude through the family to civil society. We may interpret these three stages of human development in terms of character-istic modes of behavior: independent, as each fares for himself in the original condition of solitude; cooperative, as each par-ticipates in the collective concerns of the family; competitive, as each seeks to be foremost in the struggle for economic wealth and political power in civil society. These modes of behavior reflect different motivations; if the first stage exhibits the motivational power of *amour de soi*, and the third of *amour propre*, we might ask what characterizes the motivational base of the second stage. Rousseau offers no explicit answer, but his account suggests one – *amour de la famille*, love of family.

We may also interpret these stages in terms of their charac-teristic psychological content: the original sentiment of existing within oneself; the sense of existing as part of a larger whole, the family; and the modern sentiment of existing only in the

---

7 Or "her," if we think of the original human being as female.

opinions and regard of others. On the one hand, this content relates to Rousseau's understanding of liberty: the sentiment of existing within oneself is the deepest manifestation of the adequacy of one's powers to meet one's needs and desires, and so of liberty. Whereas the sentiment of existing only in the regard of others is the parallel manifestation of the inadequacy of one's powers – it is the powers others ascribe to one that determine whether one's needs and desires are met – and so it denies one's liberty. The connection between sensing one's existence as part of a larger whole and liberty will be one of the themes of later chapters.

On the other hand, we may relate this psychological content to modes of expression: the silence of solitude; the gesture of being at home, *chez soi*; the speech of the festival and forum. But as we draw these distinctions, we need to recognize that the fault lines, as it were, that emerge from our analysis do not always fall precisely where they are represented in Rousseau's rhetoric. Recall Rousseau's account of his quarter-hour under the tree – "with what simplicity I would have demonstrated that man is naturally good and that it is from these [social] institutions alone that men become wicked." (CW5.575, OC1.1135–6) It is indeed through socialization that human beings emerge from the deep unawareness that we might characterize more as original innocence than as goodness, and acquire the comparative understanding that under the breakdown of self-sufficiency comes to be expressed as wickedness. But this socialization is not so much the product as the creator of the denaturing social institutions; socialization itself results from perfectibility, which, however much its cumulative effects alter the species, operates in the awareness and reasoning and motivation of the individual. The secular Fall that is the theme of history is not imposed on human beings from without but created from within. In locating the externalization of the self in the beginnings of speech, in the first words, *aidez-moi*, of the northern languages, I have endeavored to recapture an understanding that tends to escape from parts of Rousseau's rhetoric. And on contrasting the northern and southern languages, the speech of *aidez-moi* with the speech of *aimez-moi*, I have intended to leave room for a further understanding that will carry Rousseau beyond the emptiness of the self that exists only for the other.

He is now on his way to Vincennes, and Diderot. Making our own way, now in time rather than space, through a quarter-millennium, we may want to reflect on the history with which Rousseau has presented us from our later perspective. The political and economic changes that we think of as beginning in the later eighteenth century may seem to vitiate Rousseau's analyses. And on one level they do. I have emphasized the difference between cooperative and competitive modes of interaction. Rousseau saw the society of his time as exhibiting a fundamentally competitive mode. Without denying the benefits of cooperation, he insisted that each individual gains more by taking advantage of his fellows.[8] And there are no doubt many persons who would not only nod agreement with this judgment, but insist that the economic transformations since Rousseau's time have intensified the competitive character of society – that, after all, competition is the essence of capitalism, or free enterprise.

But the claim that competition must dominate cooperation is mistaken. Interaction is competitive insofar as gains are, and must be, balanced by losses; if the outcome of competitive interaction is not in effect a draw, leaving the parties where they were initially, then it must distinguish winners and losers. Competitive interaction is, in the parlance of economists and game theorists, *zero sum*. Interaction is cooperative insofar as gains are possible

---

[8] See Note IX (*7 in CW3) to the *Discourse on the Origin of Inequality*, where Rousseau says, "If I am answered that Society is so constituted that each man gains by serving the others, I shall reply that this would be very well, if he did not gain still more by harming them." (CW3.75, OC3.203)

all around; the outcome may reveal only winners. Cooperative interaction is *variable sum.* The secret is to structure it so that each party, motivated by considerations of its own interest, is led to act in such a way that the outcome optimally furthers the interests of all. Discovering this secret – Adam Smith's Invisible Hand – is at the core of the conceptual revolution that has transformed our understanding of society, making it possible to represent it, in John Rawls's ever-useful phrase, as "a cooperative venture for mutual advantage."[9] Contrary to Rousseau's view, society may be structured so that cooperation dominates competition.

To be sure, within the framework of cooperation, competition has a natural place. An outcome that offers gains all around may distribute those gains in quite unequal ways. Each party may seek to capture the largest possible share for itself; the task is then to arrange things so that this *distributive* competition does not undermine the prospect of an overall *productive* gain, but instead contributes to it. In a properly functioning free enterprise economy, competition for shares is structured to further the mutually beneficial productive aim. But that is another story, relevant to our purposes only in that it reflects the conceptual distance between ourselves, who do or should understand these matters, and Rousseau, who in many ways did not. Even when he recognized, as in the discovery of the arts of agriculture and metallurgy, the absolute benefits, he failed to grasp both their human significance, in enabling persons to match aptitudes with occupations, and their ongoing dynamic – the prospect of ever-continuing gains.

What Rousseau did understand, however, was the significance of positional goods which are essentially competitive. If he were able to look at the actual course of social development since his time, he might, I think, suggest that the success of modern

---

[9] John Rawls, *A Theory of Justice* (Cambridge, MA: Harvard University Press, 1971), 4.

pluralistic societies has been based on their ability to defuse positional conflict by nonpositional gains. Each person benefits absolutely by access to an increasing quantity and variety of commodities. But each person also internalizes that benefit as a positional gain, comparing his or her present situation with the *previous* situation of more favored persons. The time lag in positional perception allows real absolute gains to take on the illusion of also being positional gains.

And Rousseau would further insist that the psychological crisis he diagnosed – that human begins in society take their sentiment of existence only from the opinions and regard of others – remains deeply imbedded in our social fabric. The idea of "sociable man, always outside of himself" is the forerunner of the alienated worker in Marx, the anomic individual in Durkheim, the outer-directed man in Riesman. Rousseau is perhaps the first to diagnose a malaise at the core of the sense of self in civil society, and in this way, however much he may misunderstand some of our circumstances, he may claim to be the first to understand *us.* More persons may enjoy affluence than ever before in human history, but the price of that affluence, Rousseau will remind us, is that we have made the demand – *aidez-moi* – that is at the root of our unfreedom, our alienation from ourselves.

But my concern is primarily to read Rousseau's understanding of the human condition. The *Discourse on the Origin of Inequality,* which has provided the textual core of this first chapter, offers us a bleak account, a legend of the Fall of humankind. But for Rousseau there are other, redemptive legends, in which the Fall becomes a fortunate Fall. We must take seriously human perfectibility. Only a perfectible being can become degraded, and Rousseau has insisted on our degradation. But the positive promise of perfectibility can be realized, or so Rousseau claims.

The *Discourse on Inequality* was published in 1755, four years after the earlier *Discourse on the Sciences and Arts,* which represented the first fruits of Rousseau's illumination on the road to

Vincennes. In the next years, Rousseau turned from diagnosis to remedy, to the prospects for restoring persons to a condition of freedom. His thoughts took two very different and indeed incompatible directions. On the one hand, he proposed an educational regime that would reduce the individual's dependence on others and protect him against the destructive effects of *amour propre*. On the other hand, he proposed political institutions that would make all persons totally interdependent as parts in a social whole that would replace personal dependence with civil freedom. The results of these studies were published in 1762, in *Emile*, subtitled *On Education*, and in the *Social Contract*, or *Principles of Political Right*. They were banned in France, whence Rousseau was obliged to flee to avoid arrest, and burned in his native city, Geneva, "as unwise, scandalous, impious, tending to destroy the Christian religion and all governments." (Quoted in OC1.1565, my trans.) Their ideas will occupy the next two chapters.

2

Making a Man

"Everything is good as it leaves the hands of the Author of things; everything degenerates in the hands of man." (Bl.37, OC4.245) In these opening words of *Emile*, Rousseau reminds us of his story of the Fall. Now we must join him in making a new beginning. We shall take an infant, as yet uncorrupted by his fellows and his society, and we shall ask if he may be made a man – not one of the denatured and alienated men of Rousseau's time, or of today, not a man driven by *amour propre* to take the sentiment of his existence only from the regard of another, but a man who is "born free" (in the opening words of the *Social Contract*) and who lives as he was born.

Rousseau's conception of freedom or liberty is focused on the adequacy of each person's powers to meet his or her needs and desires. In this sense, the idea of being *born* free is not that one is able to provide adequately for oneself at birth, but rather that one is born *to* freedom – that one naturally comes to maturity as a being whose powers are adequate for his needs and desires. Our first ancestors were born to freedom, and came to it; we today are still born to freedom, but we do not come to it – as we mature, we acquire desires and passions that can be satisfied, not by our own powers, but only through the powers of our fellows. In *Emile* Rousseau asks, how can a man still come to freedom? How can he avoid acquiring the desires that would engender virulent *amour*

propre, and make him dependent on the powers and wills of his
fellows? But he asks these questions against the background of
a society in which men do not come to freedom. Rousseau asks
how a particular individual – Émile – can be protected from the
social forces that enslave his fellows.

Before we consider how Rousseau answers these questions, we
should explore briefly a further dimension to his understanding
of freedom that is not made fully clear in the *Discourse on the Origin of Inequality*. Three forms of dependence are distinguished
in Rousseau's thought: on things, on desires, and on persons.[1]
Let us consider each of these in turn. Dependence on things
is in one sense inevitable. The adequacy of our powers to meet
our needs depends on things – on the circumstances in which
we find ourselves. Rousseau supposes that there is a natural pro-
portion among circumstances, powers, and needs; human beings
are normally capable of meeting their original needs in their natural environment. Indeed, he says that "[a]ll the animals have
exactly the faculties necessary to preserve themselves." (Bl.81,
OC4.305) In adverse circumstances, these powers may be inad-
equate, and one may be unable to enjoy to the full one's liberty.
But "dependence on things . . . is from nature . . ., has no morality [and] is in no way detrimental to freedom." (Bl.85, OC4.311)
Rousseau never suggests that adverse circumstances give rise in
themselves to any form of psychological dependence, or affect
the manner in which a person senses her own existence. Quite
reasonably, he does not suppose that our sense of self is externalized in things conceived as making up the circumstances in
which we live and act.

Dependence on desires and appetites plays a more complex
role in Rousseau's thought. In the *Social Contract*, he insists that
"the impulse of appetite alone is slavery." (CW4.142, OC3.365)

---

[1] In *Emile*, Rousseau mentions only the first and last of these. (v. OC4.311) But
   the role of dependence on desires is clear in the *Social Contract*. (v. OC3.365)

Here it is important to distinguish the natural or original appetites for food, shelter, and sex – those that are needs, essential to the preservation of the individual and the species – and the appetites that are acquired in the unfolding of human perfectibility. The former, as I have already noted, are naturally proportioned to human powers and human circumstances. But the latter are potentially unbounded. As our increasing awareness expands our affective as well as our cognitive horizons, there is no reason to expect that attaining the new objects that attract us will be within the powers that we can develop, much less those that are natural or original to us. To be sure, Rousseau insists that our powers are excessive in relation to our original desires; he contrasts man with "all the animals" in the passage quoted earlier by saying that "[m]an alone has superfluous faculties." (Bl.81, OC4.305) Superfluity is a condition of perfectibility. But superfluity has its limits; desire comes to exceed powers.

When circumstances deprive us of liberty, the deprivation is, as it were, accidental. The deprivation extends only so far as the circumstances obtain. As they alter, it alters; as they improve, liberty is restored. But when our desires deprive us of liberty, by setting demands that fall outside the powers that we have or are able to attain, the deprivation is no longer accidental. True, it extends only insofar as we continue to experience the desires. But an alteration in them is an alteration in the person. In effect, one's sense of self is dependent on one's desires, so that, when they exceed one's powers, one is hostage to them. One experiences oneself as intrinsically unfulfilled. Rousseau then recognizes this dependence as a form of slavery.

But dependence on persons plays the fundamental role in Rousseau's account of our loss of liberty – whether we consider it as part of our individual lives in the modern world or as the effect of the historical realization of our perfectibility. In the first chapter, I argued that, for Rousseau, the person who speaks the first words of our northern languages, "Help me!" – *aidez-moi* – is no longer free. Rousseau tells us that "[t]he only one who does his own will is he who, in order to do it, has no need to put another's arms at the end of his own . . . . The truly free man wants only what he can do and does what he pleases. That is my fundamental maxim." (Bl.84, OC4.309) To be dependent on another person for the fulfillment of one's needs and desires is to be dependent on an alien will, a will that is by its very nature outside of oneself, beyond one's control. In such dependence, one experiences one's will as limited and constrained by a force entirely foreign to it, the will of another. The person who is dependent on desires that she lacks the power to satisfy, and who is thereby enslaved to them, is able, at least in principle, to imagine herself freed from her slavery either through losing the desires or through gaining new powers – to imagine her wants diminished or her capacities increased. But the person who is dependent on other persons and so enslaved to them is unable to imagine herself freed from her slavery – no augmentation of her powers can extend their domain to include the will of another person. To be sure, she may rule the other, compelling him to do her bidding; she may be master. But nevertheless she depends on the response of the other, which is determined by his will. Indeed, her dependence is intensified and deepened by her mastery. For in becoming master, she takes her sense of existence from being master, and requires the confirmation of being so recognized by those she dominates. This is the demand made by her *amour propre*. And the *recognition* of her mastery, the attainment of *prestige*, lies beyond her power to coerce. Her slaves may wear masks of respect and submission, as Rousseau supposes competitors wear masks of friendship, concealing their true attitudes.

Dependence on another person thus is, for Rousseau, not simply dependence on his power; most deeply, it is dependence on his recognition. It is at this point that the sentiment of existence is alienated in the other; one exists only insofar as the other recognizes one's existence. Both *that* one is, and *what* one is, are now captured by the other; one's psychological enslavement is complete. But can dependence on other persons be prevented? Can we raise "a man . . . uniquely for himself"? (Bl.41, OC4.251) Are we not seeking the chimera of a Robinson Crusoe? – and even he had his man Friday.

Émile is the boy to be raised for himself, and the task is entrusted to a Tutor. From Émile's earliest years, the Tutor is his constant companion, and it is only this constancy that permits the Tutor to perform his task. But before we examine the task, we need to know something about the person who performs it. For in Rousseau's writings the Tutor represents a recurrent figure – or rather, a union of two recurrent figures. The one is Jean-Jacques himself. Not that Rousseau thought himself fit to be a tutor in real life; he tells us that "I made a sufficient trial of this calling to be certain that I am not proper for it." (Bl.50, OC4.264) And he also tells us that he refused another offer to tutor, for fear not so much of failure as of success; the son "would no longer have wished to be a prince." (Ibid.) And so, "Not in a condition to fulfill the most useful task, I will dare at least to attempt the easier one; following the example of so many others, I shall put my hand not to the work but to the pen." (Ibid.) Émile's Tutor gives life to Rousseau's ideas; he does what Rousseau would do. He is thus an idealized Jean-Jacques, able to put into practice the principles of pedagogy that the real Rousseau can only articulate in theory. We shall encounter a different Jean-Jacques in the novel *Julie* – the pseudonymous St. Preux, also a tutor, but whose role is to express not Rousseau's idea of pedagogy but his ideal of love.

But Émile's Tutor, unlike St. Preux, is also one of Rousseau's redemptive artificers, persons who, immune themselves from denaturing, possess, or seem to possess, the power to lift their fellows from their fallen condition. In this respect the Tutor joins the Legislator of Rousseau's political writings, and Julie's husband Wolmar in his novel.[2] If we take Rousseau's opening aphorism in *Emile*, "Everything is good as it leaves the hands of the Author of things; everything degenerates in the hands of man," at face value, then we should think of these persons not as humans, but as gods, for they are represented as having the power to arrest and even to reverse the process of degeneration. And indeed they are not human insofar as their power and their existence is not explained within the framework of Rousseau's history of humankind. Rousseau never suggests that we, through our own efforts, could free ourselves from dependence on our fellows; the task must be performed for us, in the ways that we shall be examining in this and subsequent chapters. Nothing in human history itself offers redemption; in this respect Rousseau's vision clearly resembles its Christian predecessor rather than its Marxist successor.

Let us now turn to the Tutor's work. His objective is to raise a natural man, one who is "entirely for himself. He is numerical unity, the absolute whole which is relative only to itself or its kind." (Bl.39, OC4.249) His primary concerns will not be surprising, given what we have learned about Rousseau's ideas of liberty and dependence. Rousseau's "fundamental maxim," that "[t]he truly free man wants only what he can do and does what he pleases . . . need only be applied to childhood for all the rules of education to flow from it." (Bl.84, OC4.309) Émile must be protected from the unrestrained explosion of desire. His powers must be developed so that he can meet his real needs. But above all, he must be kept "in dependence only on things" (Bl.85, OC4.311), and never on persons, never on the wills of others. So

---

[2] The *Confessions* introduces a fourth artificer, Madame de Warens. But her redemptive activity is of a very different kind than that of these three, and, as will become clear later, the claims I make here about them do not apply straightforwardly to her.

far as possible, he must not find himself saying the words, "Help me!" But how can this be? For Émile exists in society, and the effects of society on the individual run entirely counter to the conditions of his freedom. Society invites, induces the unrestrained explosion of desire. It encourages the development of powers that serve, not to meet the real needs of the individual, but to fit him for social intercourse based on the desire of each person to be foremost in the recognition of others. And in so doing, it renders him dependent on the wills and opinions of others. In contrast with the numerical unity of natural man "[c]ivil man is only a fractional unity dependent on the denominator; his value is determined by his relation to . . . the social body." (Bl.39–40, OC4.249)

How to raise Émile to be natural, to enjoy natural liberty, to experience his powers as adequate to his needs and desires, to sense his own existence securely within himself, when one must recreate nature within the framework of society? How to provide him with physical and psychological self-sufficiency, and so the freedom although not the full solitude of natural man? Rousseau, in the person of the Tutor, says, "Living is the job I want to teach him . . . . All that a man should be, he will in case of need know how to be as well as anyone." (Bl.41–2, OC4.252) Émile is to be raised for independence. He cannot be literally self-sufficient, but he will learn a trade that will assure him of employment wherever and whenever he needs it. He cannot fully be spared the necessity of saying "Help me!," though he need say it only in seeking to exchange his labor in order to meet his needs. Thus he will not have developed the unbounded desires that, in Rousseau's view, lead men to enslave themselves to their fellows in the vain attempt to fulfill them. And most important of all, he will not have developed the need to find favor with other men. His talents, even if in themselves mediocre, will have been developed sufficiently that others will accept him as a useful member of society, and beyond that he will need only his own good opinion of himself to be content with his lot and his life.

Nature and education are not to be opposed in the raising of Émile. But if his education is that of nature, it is not supplied by nature. The Tutor must use all his art to raise Émile in dependence on things and not persons. As Rousseau says, "One must use a great deal of art to prevent social man [man who must live in society] from being totally artificial." (Bl.317, OC4.640) For Émile's environment must be structured in every detail if the wrong desires, the wrong dependences, are not to develop. "From the moment that the child begins to distinguish objects, it is important that there be selectivity in those one shows him." (Bl.63, OC4.282) To be sure, Rousseau insists, "Love childhood; promote its games, its pleasures, its amiable instinct." (Bl.79, OC4.302) The child is a child, and Rousseau warns against hastening its development. One should not hurry to make children talk, or give them words beyond their ideas. Indeed, Rousseau says, "What must be done is to prevent anything from being done" (Bl.41, OC4.251) – anything that would interfere with, or anticipate, the development of nature. "If you could do nothing and let nothing be done, if you could bring your pupil healthy and robust to the age of twelve without his knowing how to distinguish his right hand from his left, at your first lessons the eyes of his understanding would open up to reason." (Bl.93, OC4.323) This may be beyond even the Tutor's powers, but even a lesser degree of prevention is no easy task, and correction, should matters go amiss, poses difficulties which require that the Tutor have the most complete control possible over the child's environment.

Thus Rousseau describes a stratagem he claims to have employed himself when temporarily caring for a tyrannical child. The child was bored – "I had arranged for that." (Bl.123, OC4.367) Rousseau was, or seemed, busy; the child demanded to be taken for a walk. Rousseau refused. The child announced his intention to go for a walk alone; Rousseau let him. Ill at ease, but unwilling to back down, the child set out. "This was just what I was waiting for. *Everything was prepared in advance* [emphasis mine] . . . . Hardly had the child taken a few steps before he heard, right and left, remarks about him. 'Neighbor, look at the pretty monsieur! Where is he going all alone? He is going to get lost . . . .' . . . A bit farther on he met up with some rascals of about his age who provoked him and jeered at him . . . . Alone and without protection, he saw himself everybody's plaything . . . . Meanwhile one of my friends . . . was following him step by step without his noticing it, and accosted him when the time was right." (Bl.123–4, OC4.367–8)

To structure Émile's environment so that nothing interferes with the course of nature requires his entire dependence on the Tutor. Since nature has been banished from society, the Tutor's will must serve as substitute, so that what happens to Émile must be and must be *only* what the Tutor wills to happen. And yet Émile must remain entirely independent of others and their wills – and so of the will of the Tutor. How is this possible? How can Émile be at once totally dependent on the Tutor and yet dependent only on things and never on the wills of other persons? How can an education that requires complete dependence bring Émile to independence?

Rousseau is well aware that overcoming this apparent contradiction is the task that he has set the Tutor – or if you like, has set himself. He begins with the idea of "well-regulated freedom." (Bl.92, OC4.321) Émile knows nothing of "the laws of the possible and the impossible . . . they can be expanded and contracted around him as one wants." (Ibid.) The Tutor must be the master, and "[y]ou will not be the child's master if you are not the master of all that surrounds him." (Bl.95, OC4.325) Rousseau's insistence on total control is clear. But this is not how things are to appear to Émile. His dependence must appear to him as independence. He may see no will opposed to or affecting his own, so that the Tutor's contrivances must appear to him as the natural course of events. The Tutor intends him to go for a walk, but he thinks the walk his own idea; the Tutor plans the encounters with others that seem to him a matter of chance. Rousseau makes this fully explicit when he advises, "Take an opposite route with your pupil. Let him always believe that he is the master, and let it always be you who are. There is no subjection so perfect as that which keeps the appearance of freedom. Thus the will itself is made captive." (Bl.120, OC4.362)

The captivity of the will is at the core of Rousseau's account of education. For this captivity enables him to reconcile the requirement that the pupil be absolutely dependent on the Tutor, with the requirement that the pupil never experience subjection to or dependence on the wills of others. Essentially, by capturing his pupil's will, the Tutor *internalizes* his own will in the pupil. Émile experiences, as the dictates of his own will, what the Tutor has ordained.

Do you not dispose . . . of everything which surrounds him? Are you not the master of affecting him as you please? Are not his labors, his games, his pleasures, his pains, all in your hands without his knowing it? Doubtless he ought to do only what he wants; but he ought to want only what you want him to do. He ought not to make a step without your having foreseen it; he ought not to open his mouth without your knowing what he is going to say. (Bl.120, OC4.362–3)

We shall return shortly to this last, surely chilling, sentence.

The Tutor asks,

You cannot imagine how Émile can be docile at twenty? . . . It has taken fifteen years of care to contrive this hold for myself . . . . It is true that I leave him the appearance of independence, but he was never better subjected to me; for now he is subjected because he wants to be. As long as I was unable to make myself master of his will, I remained master of his person; I was never a step away from him. Now I sometimes leave him to himself, because I govern him always. (Bl.332, OC4.661)

And how does Émile respond? As he comes to maturity, we hear him saying to the Tutor,

I want to obey your laws; I want to do so always. This is my steadfast will. If ever I disobey you, it will be in spite of myself. Make me free by protecting me against those of my passions which do violence to me. Prevent me from being their slave; force me to be my own master and to obey not my senses but my reason. (Bl.325, OC4.651–2)

The trick is done; Émile has internalized the Tutor's will. He does this by identifying his own will with what he understands as the Tutor's laws. As I shall discuss in the next chapter, Rousseau makes clear in the *Social Contract* that dependence on law is the antithesis of dependence on will, so that it restores rather than destroys freedom. But what is important for us to note now is that although Émile has come to represent his relation to the Tutor in terms of law, even this relation requires the language of *making* ("Make me free") and *forcing* ("force me to be my own master"). We may question whether Émile's will is fully one with the Tutor's.

Is Émile free? Has the Tutor succeeded in bringing Émile to independence through dependence? Let us reflect on that remarkable sentence, "He ought not to make a step without your having foreseen it; he ought not to open his mouth without your knowing what he is going to say." For it has an almost exact parallel in another of Rousseau's writings – a very different work, the *Dialogues*, subtitled *Rousseau Judge of Jean-Jacques*.[3]

Most of Rousseau's later writings are exercises in understanding himself, and, as I shall argue, understanding human nature in his own person. The *Confessions* and the *Reveries* are the best known of these, but between them comes a very different form

---

[3] Jean Starobinski is, to my knowledge, the first to call attention to this parallel. See *Jean-Jacques Rousseau: Transparency and Obstruction* (Chicago and London: University of Chicago Press, 1988), 217.

of self-examination, the darkest of all Rousseau's writings, the *Dialogues*. As he turned decisively in his own thinking from the Enlightenment views of the Encyclopedists, and as he distanced himself even further from the orthodoxies of church and court, he became the object of real and widespread animosity in many intellectual quarters, including some whose members had once been among his friends. Rousseau, always overly sensitive to rejection, magnified this into the paranoid vision of a universal plot against him, a plot that, he imagined, had so well succeeded that even those who still seemed to be friends were concealed enemies, and among the populace at large he was considered a monster, "the horror of the human race." (CW1.36, OC1.705) The *Dialogues* record a series of conversations about Jean-Jacques, the supposed monster, between a Frenchman who initially believes the reports that have been spread of his infamy, and a character called Rousseau, who at the outset is appalled by the crimes of which the Frenchman has just been informing him, yet is unable to reconcile them with the views expressed in the works by Jean-Jacques that he has read. In the course of the *Dialogues*, Rousseau agrees to meet Jean-Jacques in person, the Frenchman to read his writings, and the two come to be of a very different mind. They resolve to seek Jean-Jacques' friendship and to preserve what they can of his writings from the enemies who would destroy or misuse them.

In the first of the three *Dialogues*, much is said about these enemies, the persons, often referred to as "*nos Messieurs*" – "our gentlemen" – who have claimed to unmask Jean-Jacques, revealing his supposed crimes to the world. These nameless, faceless persons,[4] who rule Jean-Jacques' destiny, are at the center of the universal plot. And among what is said of them is that "[t]hey took precautions that are no less effective by keeping him under such surveillance he cannot say a word that is not recorded nor

---

[4] Their identities are never revealed in the *Dialogues*.

take a step that is not noted, nor formulate a plan that is not seen through the moment it is conceived." (CW1.36, OC1.706) And again, "[H]e [Jean-Jacques] can neither say a word, nor take a step, nor lift a finger unless they know it and want it." (CW1.39–40, OC1.710) And now recall the Tutor's words, speaking of Émile's situation: "He ought not to make a step without your having foreseen it; he ought not to open his mouth without your knowing what he is going to say." Not a step, not a word. Émile keeps "the appearance of freedom." (Bl.120, OC4.362) Jean-Jacques "appears to be free." (CW1. 36, OC1.706) Did Rousseau recognize the echoes?

How is the appearance of liberty maintained? I have sketched Rousseau's stratagem in dealing with the tyrannical child. *Emile* is replete with other stratagems. The Tutor, Jean-Jacques (since Rousseau uses his own name), suggests a walk to Émile. They get lost, or so it seems to the boy. "He does not know we are at the gate of Montmorency and that a simple copse hides it from us." (Bl.181, OC4.449) They are hungry. The Tutor pretends not to know what to do. By skillful questioning about the child's previous knowledge of the direction from Montmorency to the forest, and about determining directions from the shadow cast by the sun, Émile is led to head them in the right direction. The stratagem may seem innocuous, but the contrivance remains concealed. Émile seems to find his way freely through a natural obstacle, but he does not find the Tutor, presenting and removing that obstacle.

Émile and the Tutor attend a fair, where "a magician attracts a wax duck floating in a tub of water with a piece of bread." (Bl.173, OC4.437) At home, they imitate the trick with a magnet. They return to the fair, and the boy confounds the magician by imitating him. The magician invites them to return the next day; Émile arranges for all his friends to witness. But now the magician confounds the boy; the duck obeys only its master. The next day the magician visits Émile, explains the trick, and delivers a

rebuke to the Tutor for letting Émile try to "discredit his games
and take away his livelihood." (Bl.174, OC4.439) They attend the
magician's next performance – "If my pupil dared so much as to
open his mouth, he would deserve to be annihilated." (Bl.175,
OC4.440) Do we need Rousseau's footnote to tell us "that this little scene was arranged and that the magician had been instructed
about the role he had to play"? (Bl.487, OC4.1420) Do we find
this scene so innocuous?

And now consider the stratagems used by "our gentlemen" in
their dealings with that other Jean-Jacques.

In taking the greatest care to deprive him of all his friends, they were
especially asked always to keep up the appearance and title of friend,
and to maintain the same tone in deceiving him as they had previously
used to welcome him. It is his guilty suspiciousness alone that makes
him unhappy. Without that, he would be a little more taken in, but he
would live as happily as before. (CW1.40, OC1.711)

They have made arrangements so that while he appears to be free among
men, he has no real society with them; so that he lives alone in the crowd;
so that he knows nothing of what is done, nothing of what is said around
him, nothing especially of what concerns and interests him most; so that
he feels completely encumbered with chains of which he can neither
show nor see the least vestige. (CW1.36, OC1.706)

And in doing all this, "what is great, generous, admirable in our
Gentlemen's plan, [is] . . . that in preventing him from following
his wishes and accomplishing his evil designs, they still seek to
obtain the sweet things of life for him, so that he finds what he
needs everywhere and what he could misuse nowhere." (CW1.44,
OC1.715–16)

When we read the various stratagems that the Tutor is ready
to employ in raising Émile, we recognize that the real difference between his situation and the one ascribed in the *Dialogues*
to Jean-Jacques is only that Émile feels himself his own master,
whereas Jean-Jacques feels himself enslaved, albeit by invisible,
intangible chains. "[Our Gentlemen] have built walls of darkness

around him through which he cannot see; they have buried him alive among the living." (CW1.36, OC1.706) We must ask later why Jean-Jacques feels enslaved, what causes his "guilty suspiciousness." But here I want simply to draw the comparison, to note that the education of Émile, and the entombment of the wretched Jean-Jacques, employ the same means, and require the same mastery.

The work of the Tutor is an exercise in total control. In Rousseau's paranoid vision of the exercise of such control over Jean-Jacques, its real significance appears. The Tutor claims to make Émile a natural man, free, independent of any alien will. This freedom can be attained only through the capture and transformation of Émile's will. But Rousseau's sense of utter dependence on "our Gentlemen," however exaggerated it may be, reflects his deep rejection of this so-called freedom, and calls into question the educational theory that defends it. In the *Dialogues*, he speaks of "this feigned freedom." (CW1.39, OC1.710) Does he know that he is speaking of the freedom of Émile?

Perhaps not. We need not suppose that Rousseau was consciously insincere in representing the Tutor's aim as that of making Émile a self-sufficient individual, able to live, physically and psychologically, within himself. Nor need we suppose that he grasped consciously the real effect of the Tutor's methods, which offered Émile subjective independence – the appearance of liberty – at the price of objective dependence. (It would, however, seem that Émile comes to recognize that his independence is obtained at the price of dependence: "force me to be my own master," we have heard him tell the Tutor.) But my claim is that Rousseau's lack of conscious awareness of the real nature of the Tutor and his relationship with Émile conceals his unconscious awareness, which is expressed in the *Dialogues*. They make explicit the totalitarian reality implicit in the idea that "the will is made captive." Thus they contain Rousseau's own critique of the Tutor's educational methods, even though it is a critique of which he never becomes consciously aware.

When Émile reaches manhood, it is time for him to marry. This, as all else, is arranged by the Tutor. He has long talked to Émile of his future beloved, calling her, laughingly, "Sophie" (Bl.329, OC4.657), and encouraging him to search for her where, as he says, "I was quite sure she was not to be found." (Bl.354, OC4.691) But at last the time has come, and the appropriate girl, a real Sophie, is discovered as if by accident.

Sophie is a troubling presence. Rousseau's first words about her are, "Sophie ought to be a woman as Émile is a man." (Bl.357, OC4.692) And woman, he tells us, "is made specially to please man," and indeed "to be subjugated." (Bl.358, OC4.693) Rousseau follows this thought through to its moral conclusion – "Opinion is the grave of virtue among men and its throne among women." (Bl.365, OC4.702–3) To depend on opinion is to depend on others for one's sentiment of existence. It is to be alienated from oneself. It is the grave of man's virtue, the mark of his fallen condition. But the fall of Adam, it would seem, is not the fall of Eve. In depending for her sentiment of existence first on her father, and then on her husband, she is fulfilling her nature. But what nature can this be? There is a contradiction at the heart of Rousseau's account of woman; she is human, but she is not born to be free.

And since she is not born to be free, Sophie's education will be very different from Émile's. Rousseau does not mince words here. "[W]hat is thought of her is no less important to her than what she actually is. From this it follows that the system of woman's education ought to be contrary in this respect to the system of our education." (Bl. 364–5, OC4.702) Girls "ought to be constrained very early" so that "it never costs them anything to tame all their caprices in order to submit them to the wills of others." (Bl.369, OC4.709) The elaborate program that the Tutor must follow to keep Émile from coming to depend on the opinions of his fellows would not merely be wasted on Sophie; it would be entirely detrimental to her development. Her instructor must constantly impress the opinions of others upon her, so that she learns to make them her first concern.

In the *Social Contract*, Rousseau insists that the family is the only natural form of society. In the *Discourse on Inequality*, as I noted in the first chapter, the era of the family is shown as the happiest and stablest of human epochs. But since Rousseau insists that the husband must rule, and that the wife must depend on his opinion, since he insists that the husband must control his wife's conduct so that he may be assured of the paternity of her children, it clearly follows that the family is based on the dependence of women. Women must lose their liberty at an earlier stage in human history than men. But does Rousseau recognize this, or treat it as loss? Consciously, he seeks to restore man's freedom, but he seeks no similar redemption for woman. Unconsciously, his depiction of the miserable Jean-Jacques may be a recognition and rejection of the servitude of Émile, but there is no corresponding depiction that would reveal the very different but no less real servitude of Sophie, which Rousseau seems simply to accept.

We shall reexamine Rousseau's account of women when we have considered his portrayal of Julie in his novel and of Madame de Warens in the *Confessions*. Here let us simply return to our story, with the contradiction in Rousseau's account of women unresolved. Sophie is found. Courtship ensues. Enforced absence, required by the Tutor, makes the hearts grow fonder. Marriage follows, with the hand of the Tutor surprisingly visible in controlling the new couple's access to the nuptial bed. Nor does he bid farewell to his pupil, for he relates, "A few months later Émile enters my room one morning, embraces me, and says, 'My master, congratulate your child. He hopes soon to have the honour of being a father.'" (Bl.480, OC4.867) And Émile continues, "Advise us and govern us. We shall be docile. As long as I live, I shall need you. I need you more than ever now that my functions as a man begin." (Bl.480, OC4.867–8) In these last remarks, Émile explicitly acknowledges what has been true from the outset, that his very being is dependent on the Tutor. As a child he was kept unaware of his dependence, but the silent plea that defined his relation with the Tutor may be found in those words that should now be familiar to us, *aidez-moi*. And in repeating them as his duties as husband and father begin, Émile acknowledges that he is not the true natural man, raised to a condition of self-sufficiency, but the permanent dependent of the Tutor.

Aidez-moi cannot be unsaid. I want now to turn to those other, even earlier words – the first words of the southern languages, *aimez-moi*. For *Emile* offers an account of love, although not, let me warn at the outset, Rousseau's only account, and not, I shall argue later, his deepest account. And we may also find in the unfinished sequel, *Emile and Sophie, or the Solitaries*, grounds for reflection on when the words of love are misspoken.

When Émile's heart "opens itself to the first fires of love," we are immediately told that "[i]ts sweet illusions make him a new universe of delight and enjoyment." (Bl.419, OC4.782) The mention of "illusions" should put us on our guard, for Rousseau has previously said, "Your freedom and your power extend only so far as your natural strength, and not beyond. All the rest is only slavery, illusion, and prestige."[5] (Bl.83, OC4.308) Is love then, like aid, another of the enemies of liberty?

Before we can begin to answer this, we must consider how the Tutor understands the illusions of love. When he first tells Émile that his heart needs a companion, he also speaks – but to the reader – of love. "And what is true love itself if it is not chimera, lie, and illusion? We love the image we make for ourselves far

---

[5] Bloom tr., "deception."

more than we love the object to which we apply it. If we saw what we love exactly as it is, there would be no more love on earth." (Bl.329, OC4.656) His words are echoed elsewhere, in Rousseau's Second Preface to his novel *Julie*– "Love is but illusion; it fashions for itself, so to speak, another Universe; it surrounds itself with objects that do not exist, or to which it alone has given being . . . . It can see nothing but Paradise . . . the delights of the celestial abode." (CW6.10, OC2.15–16)

Love is illusion, but the illusion is not condemned. The Tutor has more to say.

In love everything is only illusion. I admit it. But what is real are the sentiments for the truly beautiful with which love animates us and which it makes us love. This beauty is not in the object one loves; it is the work of our errors. So, what of it? Does the lover any the less sacrifice all of his low sentiments to this imaginary model? . . . Does he detach himself any the less from the baseness of the human *I*? Where is the true lover who is not ready to immolate himself for his beloved . . .? (Bl.391, OC4.743)

Love as possession of the affections of the beloved is transcended and idealized; it becomes love of the truly beautiful. The role of illusion is then to enable the lover to see the truly beautiful in his beloved.

The Tutor's final advice about love to Émile draws the explicit implication of this account. "Do you want, then, to live happily and wisely? Attach your heart only to imperishable beauty. . . . You will possess them [fragile, perishable goods] without their possessing you; and you will feel that man, who can keep nothing, enjoys only what he knows how to lose." (Bl.446, OC4.820) Émile may love Sophie, but he must not allow himself to be possessed by her.

This is love as the Tutor understands it. And not only the Tutor, for we find this view of love again in the Second Preface to *Julie*. But I consider it suspect. Even the Tutor is not at one with himself in insisting that the lover not let himself be possessed by what he loves, unless it be imperishable beauty. For he has previously spoken quite differently about possession.[6] "He who said, 'I possess Laïs without her possessing me,' uttered a witless phrase. Possession which is not reciprocal is nothing. It is at most possession of the sexual organ, not of the individual." (Bl.349, OC4.684) I shall argue that joint possession, of lover and beloved, is central to Rousseau's deepest and final view of love, bringing the evidence of both *Julie* itself (in opposition to the Second Preface) and Rousseau's confessional writings to support my claim. But it is the Tutor's view that we must suppose informs Rousseau's account of Émile's relationship with Sophie.

And this relationship proves to be a troubled one. When we leave them at the end of *Emile*, all seems well – the happy couple about to become parents. But when we rejoin them in the unfinished sequel, *Emile and Sophie*, we find their happiness to have been short-lived. The Tutor – needed "more than ever," in Émile's last words – is absent, whether dead or departed. The young couple move to Paris; their daughter dies. They no longer sense their existence as one, but as two. Sophie becomes pregnant by another man; Émile leaves. A series of misadventures brings him to captivity and enslavement by the Barbary pirates. The manuscript breaks off. Rousseau seems to have envisaged a happy ending, in which Émile and Sophie would finally be solitaries together. But what he wrote cruelly reveals the failure of the Tutor's efforts to raise someone who could carry out the duties of man's estate in the world, while preserving his natural independence.

And it reveals more. For the relationship between Émile and Sophie, as it begins in *Emile*, and continues in *Emile and Sophie*,

[6] The contrast between the Tutor's two remarks about possession has been noted by P. D. Jimack (v. notes in OC2.1678–9).

is, as I have suggested, one of Rousseau's studies of those other words, *aimez-moi*. As we proceed, we shall find that they express our dependence and determine our sentiment of existence at a level even deeper than does *aidez-moi*. In depicting the Tutor's sway as extending to love, then, Rousseau treats it as affecting the true core of Émile's being. But we should read the failure of Émile and Sophie's marriage as expressing the implicit recognition that love cannot be within the Tutor's power. We have already heard him call love "chimera, lie, and illusion," insisting that what is real in our sentiments relates us to the ideal, which we persistently misidentify with the beloved. The true implications of this view of love appear in the misfortunes of Émile and Sophie. The love that the Tutor creates does not relate the lovers to each other, but to a supposed ideal of true beauty that each mistakenly thinks he or she finds in the other. If love determines our sentiment of existence, then lovers would come to sense their existence, not in the real beloved, but in the illusory beauty they ascribe to the beloved. In representing love between persons as illusion, the Tutor makes the love between persons an instrument of alienation rather than redemption. Under his guidance the words of love are misspoken.

As I have said, I shall find another account of love in Rousseau. With that account before us, we shall be in a position to ask whether there is a way to speak the words of love that avoids illusion. We shall ask whether asking for love enchains or liberates. For the present, we should note only that *if* the Tutor's account of love were Rousseau's final word, then *aimez-moi*, like *aidez-moi*, would be words of enslavement, relating the individual to what he recognizes as other. In subsequent chapters we shall be asking whether either the demand for help or the demand for love can direct an individual not to what is alien to himself, but to what he identifies with as his truest self, the core of his sentiment of existence.

It is time to say our farewells to Émile.[7] We have followed him from infancy to captivity. Whatever his future may hold, we have not found him the man who, although in the midst of society, could maintain a largely self-sufficient life, with his sentiment of existence firmly centered in himself. The Tutor has not succeeded; he has not educated a man "for himself." The independence he has offered is only appearance, the love only illusion. But is this a fair assessment? May we not find a different message in the book – a message that puts to one side the dubious stratagems of the Tutor and the pronouncements of his mastery in favor of the clear injunctions to "be humane" (Bl.79, OC4.302) and to "(o)bserve nature" (Bl.47, OC4.259),

[7] But before we do, there is one further problem that *Emile and Sophie* raises. For it would seem that the Tutor has also failed to give Émile a proper understanding of liberty. I noted earlier that Rousseau treats dependence on things as natural and as no impediment to freedom. Indeed, he lays down the rule, "Keep the child in dependence only on things." (Bl.85, OC4.311) But when Émile comes to reflect on his situation as a slave, he expresses a totally different and opposed view. "Was I not born slave to necessity? What new bonds can men impose on me? . . . The only true servitude is that of nature." (OC4.916–7, my trans.) And he concludes this reflection with the thought, "In order not to be reduced to nothingness, I must be moved by another's will instead of by my own." In his subsequent conduct, he makes his master's long-term profit the basis of his successful appeal against an overseer who is working him and his fellow slaves to death. We may admire his ingenuity (albeit suspecting that in the real world he would hardly have succeeded so easily), but we can hardly fail to be aware that Émile is reduced to depending for his very existence on being able to elicit the favorable judgment – in effect, the recognition – of another. And yet Émile pronounces himself "freer than before"! (OC4.916)

Of course I do not intend to suggest that Émile should have chosen to go to his death rather than accept his dependence on his master and try to work that dependence to his advantage. My point is that Émile fails to recognize that his circumstances are incompatible with his being free – just as, Rousseau supposes, the circumstances of persons in society are incompatible with their being free. Émile embraces a quite different conception of freedom than Rousseau's. If we accept Rousseau's conception, then Émile deceives himself about his real lack of freedom – just as persons in society deceive themselves. But the text shows no recognition of this. Perhaps Rousseau himself is deceived?

and the call to respect the child and the ways in which children naturally develop in designing their education? May we not agree with Rousseau's emphasis on freedom, and find, in his insistence that the child be dependent on things and not on persons, the recognition that what should be learned is not to respond to the prohibitions and rewards that others may employ for their own purposes, but to respond to the constraints and opportunities that the world itself presents? Even if the means he proposes sometimes subvert his ends, should we not applaud the ends?

But the question is not one of applause. We might like to think that Rousseau has understood the true objective of education but has erred in his choice of means to realize it. But this ignores the question whether the objective is such that the choice of means must fail to realize it, and instead accomplish the very opposite of what seems to be intended. Rousseau offers us a thought experiment, and not a real exercise in educational engineering, but it provides a very clear illustration of the idea that human beings may achieve liberation through control. He concludes *Emile* with the experiment's apparent success. But if, as I have claimed, this appearance conceals the reality of failure, a failure that Rousseau himself implicitly recognizes, then we must ask whether this failure lies in the particular means – the particular ways in which control is exercised, or in the type of means, the use of control in any form, *or* in the very idea that there are means, that liberation is a possible objective.

If Rousseau's account of humankind's loss of freedom is sound, then he is surely right to believe that only the most radical measures could enable an individual man to escape our common Fall. If the social world in which we live leads each of us to sense his or her existence only in the regard of our fellows, then the measures that would prevent this must extend to control over the formative experiences that shape our sense of existence. The Tutor's control is needed to prevent Émile from engaging in "free" social interaction with his fellows, because such interaction

would be destructive of Émile's own freedom. And it is exactly
this control that the Tutor exercises in taking Émile's will captive.
But it is equally this control that justifies us – and, unconsciously,
Rousseau – in treating the Tutor's task as equivalent to the plot of
"our Gentlemen." The Tutor has not gone astray in the *particular*
measures of control that he has employed to keep Émile from
the alienated existence of his fellows. For Rousseau, it is the very
project of individual liberation through control that proves fundamentally flawed, and flawed in ways that his paranoia enables
him to express.

I remember from my childhood a hymn that begins, "Make me
a captive, Lord, / And then I shall be free." There is a widespread
pattern exemplified here; one is freed, or so it is claimed, from
enslaving dependence by transferring that dependence to an
allegedly liberating power. The believer is freed from sin and
worldly concerns in becoming dependent on God. We find this
pattern in cults, in psychoanalysis, and in communism. This last
introduces the politics of dependence – the worker is freed from
his exploitation by the capitalist through becoming dependent
on the vanguard, the party. And political, collective dependence
will be one of the themes of the next chapter.

But my theme here has been individual dependence. Émile
is saved from dependence on his fellows by being kept from
them – if not in appearance, yet in reality – and this isolation is
accomplished through his dependence on the Tutor. Rousseau
constructs the argument of his book around the transfer pattern. But as I have argued, Rousseau then, consciously or unconsciously, deconstructs the argument in *Emile and Sophie*, and the
Dialogues. I claimed in the first chapter that Rousseau is perhaps
the first modern thinker to understand us as alienated from our
true selves. I want now to make a further claim – that he is the
first modern thinker to show an awareness of the contradiction
at the heart of those endeavors, social and political, religious and
therapeutic, that seek to overcome our alienation by transferring

our dependence. But his awareness is largely implicit. Explicitly, he presents himself as advocate rather than critic, identifying himself with the Tutor in the endeavor to make a man, to bring Émile to maturity in the freedom to which he is born.

And indeed, if we ask, which is the true Rousseau, the advocate or the critic, we must reply that only by understanding the presence of both advocate and critic can we hope to understand him, whether as man or as thinker. The distinguished Swiss critic Jean Starobinski has written of Rousseau in terms of "transparency and obstruction."[8] Rousseau is ever seeking and proclaiming transparency – Émile is to be the man transparent to himself, aware of his self-contained existence. But Rousseau is ever finding obstruction – Émile's real existence is the deliberately concealed work of the Tutor. The transparency is illusion.

Making a man ends in failure. But there is an alternative, mentioned at the beginning of *Emile* by Rousseau himself. "Forced to combat nature or the social institutions, one must choose between making a man or a citizen, for one cannot make both at the same time." (Bl.39, OC4.248) Social institutions have deprived man of his natural freedom. Can these institutions restore freedom? Can each person's relation to his fellows be reconstituted so that each no longer depends on the alien other for his sense of self? Is it possible, in other words, to make a citizen? Émile could not unsay "Help me!"; in the next chapter I shall ask if saying these words may instead be transformed.

---

[8] See the reference in note 3 above.

3

Politics of Redemption

"At the moment of that reading I saw another universe and I became another man." (CW5.294, OC1.351) In these words Rousseau announced his transformation under the tree on the way to Vincennes. We have examined some of the fruits of that transformation – the legends of the Fall recounted in the *Discourse on the Origin of Inequality*, the attempt to make a free man in *Emile*. But we have not asked, who is this other man whom Rousseau became as he read the question of the Academy of Dijon, "Has the restoration of the Sciences and Arts tended to purify or corrupt Morals?"

Rousseau's illumination took place in the summer of 1749. The following January he wrote to Voltaire, signing himself "J. J. Rousseau, citoyen de Genève." It was his first declaration of his new identity. He published his prize-winning answer to the Academy's question, the *Discourse on the Sciences and Arts*, not under his own name but "Par un Citoyen de Genève." He came to be familiarly called and identified as "the Citizen," and several of his subsequent writings were identified as by "J. J. [or, alternatively, Jean Jacques] Rousseau, citoyen de Genève." Citizen of Geneva – this is the identity Rousseau assumes under the tree on the way to Vincennes. It is the Citizen who speaks in the writings we have examined in previous chapters, and who should reveal himself directly as we consider Rousseau's ideal of citizenship – his ideal of what he claims to be.

In this chapter, we shall examine that ideal. We shall see how Rousseau develops it in his principal political writings. Later, when we turn to Rousseau's autobiographical works, we shall have to ask how the ideal of the citizen relates to the Citizen of Geneva – the person Rousseau claims to have become in reading the words of the *Mercury of France*. We shall not find this relationship a harmonious one. Indeed, having examined some of the false identities that served Rousseau as disguises, we shall ask if the Citizen is among their number.

But let us now hear the Citizen of Geneva speak to us about the citizen. We begin at the beginning of the *Social Contract*: "Man was/is born free, and everywhere he is in chains. One who believes himself the master of others is nonetheless a greater slave than they. How did this change occur? I do not know. What can make it legitimate? I believe I can resolve[1] this question." (CW4.131, OC3.351) What Rousseau professes that he does not know is, of course, what he has already told us in the *Discourse on Inequality*. We know how a race of free beings has come to be a race of slaves, in coming to depend on their fellows not only for the material conditions of their existence, but for their very sense of self. We know how each man, born to freedom, has come to wear the shackles of society. But in the *Social Contract*, this knowledge is irrelevant. What we must now learn is how Rousseau legitimizes dependence, for this is exactly what he claims to be able to do. The task may seem impossible. But we should note what Rousseau says in *Emile* about making a citizen – "one wants to raise him [a man] for others." (Bl.39, OC4.248) Men have ceased to exist for themselves. If this loss cannot be prevented, can it be accepted and transformed?

---

[1] Bush tr., "answer."

If we are to understand Rousseau's view of the making of a citizen, we need to juxtapose two stories. The first is the familiar account in the sixth, seventh, and eighth chapters of Book I of the *Social Contract*, in which he explains the social compact, the sovereign, and the civil state. The second is the account of the work of the Legislator, in the seventh chapter of Book II, supplemented by the brief reference to the citizen at the beginning of *Emile*, and his account of educating citizens. Civic education is a central theme of the *Discourse on Political Economy*, an essay Rousseau published in Diderot's famous *Encyclopedia* in 1755 – the same year that he published the *Discourse on the Origin of Inequality*. And Rousseau returned to this subject in one of his last works, unpublished in his lifetime, the *Considerations on the Government of Poland*, written in 1771–2 at the request of the Polish Count Wielhorski. Once we have seen how the citizen is formed, we may look specifically at how Rousseau related his ideal of citizenship to Geneva, a subject he treats in the Epistle Dedicatory to the *Discourse on Inequality*, and to which he returns in *Letters from the Mountain*.

"I assume that men have reached the point where obstacles to their self-preservation in the state of nature prevail by their resistance over the forces each individual can use to maintain himself in that state." (CW4.138, OC3.360) Each man says "Help me!" – *aidez-moi*. The original adequacy of powers to needs has disappeared; Rousseau does not here consider how or why. Were human beings not to change their way of life, they would perish; what change will enable them to survive? They must combine their forces, "set them to work by a single motivation; and make them act in concert." (Ibid.) But how may an individual combine his forces with others, without sacrificing his liberty? Rousseau asks exactly this question: how may each unite with his fellows so that he may enjoy the protection of their united forces, but so that he "obeys only himself and remains as free as before"? (Ibid.) How may each depend on the powers of his fellows and yet not be enslaved to them? There is but one way, he insists: "the total alienation of each associate, with all his rights, to the whole community." (Ibid.) This is the core of Rousseau's social compact.

We may find this answer disturbing. How does this total alienation differ from "the last degree of inequality" – the emergence of arbitrary power – that Rousseau describes in the *Discourse on Inequality*, where "all individuals become equals again because they are nothing"? (CW3.65, OC3.191) Rousseau's answer turns, not on the extent of each person's submission, for in both cases each submits totally, but on the recipient of that submission – in the *Discourse* "the will of the Master . . . [who has no] other rule except his passions" (ibid.), but in the *Social Contract* the general will. For the general will is the fundamental legitimating device in Rousseau's political thought. Although some have found it a mysterious notion, investing it with a metaphysical status that seems to me no part of Rousseau's thought, I suggest that we understand the general will as no more than the translation of the shared grounds of association into common directives for action. Human beings come together so that they may use their combined forces to defend and protect each person and his goods; the general will translates that shared intent into the actions that its fulfillment requires. The totality of each individual's alienation of his person and rights assures that each is equally placed, and that no one reserves any portion of his forces to protect himself against or in opposition to his fellows, rather than in harmony with them. Each is free, because the combined powers of his fellows are adequate to preserve and maintain him; the balance of needs and powers has been restored.

"Each of us puts his person and all his power in common under the supreme direction of the general will; and in a body we receive each member as an indivisible part of the whole." (CW4.139, italics omitted; OC3.361) Thus is created a collective body, the republic or body politic, "which receives from this same act its unity, its common *self*, its life, and its will." (Ibid.) But if each is to identify with this collective body, then he must participate in the formation of its will. For him to consider the general will as his own, he must see it as emanating from himself and not from some alien source. As an active body, the republic exercises sovereignty, which is nothing but the formulation and realization of the general will, and expresses itself in law. Each citizen must therefore participate in the exercise of sovereignty, and this participation binds him to the whole. This is the central tenet of Rousseau's political theory, and as I shall show later, it arises out of his understanding of the status he shares with his fellow citizens of Geneva.

The general will comes from all and applies to all. It differs from the will of all, which is the mere aggregate of individual wills, with neither a common basis nor a common object. (v. OC3.371) The general will is the will of each in his capacity as citizen, a capacity that unites him with his fellows in the community, and it is addressed to each in that same capacity. This dual generality ensures that no individual can be singled out from the others by the expression of the general will. The edicts of the general will – the laws – treat each person as an inseparable part of an indivisible whole. It is thus through the general will that the identification of each citizen with the society as a whole is established.

But Rousseau must recognize that "each individual can, as a man, have a private will contrary to or differing from the general will he has as a Citizen." (CW4.140–1, OC3.363) Even though he has alienated himself to the community and participates in the formation of its will, he retains a "private interest [that] can speak to him quite differently from the common interest. His absolute and naturally independent existence can bring him to view what he owes the common cause as a free contribution, the loss of which will harm others less than its payment burdens him." (CW4.141, OC3.363) To meet the threat to society posed by each person's private interest, Rousseau insists that "whoever refuses to obey the general will shall be constrained to do so by the entire body; which means only that he will be forced to be free. For this is the condition that, by giving each Citizen to the fatherland [*la patrie*], guarantees him against all personal dependence." (CW4.141, OC3.364)

The concern that Rousseau addresses here should be evident, however we may judge his manner of addressing it. Human beings must unite to survive; they can unite to be ruled by a master, or they can unite to exercise together the general will. Only the latter avoids *personal* dependence – and does so in two ways, by preventing one's dependence *on* a particular person, but also, since the general will must *apply* equally to all, by preventing one's dependence *as* a particular person. And so the conformity of each to the dictates of the general will may be seen as necessary to liberty. But is it sufficient? Is one free insofar as one depends on the general will – on the collective body of the republic? Is one free if one must be *forced* to recognize and adhere to the general will? No doubt the citizen who truly identifies himself with the general will also identifies with its requirements, and so does not consider them incompatible with his own liberty. But the person who must be "forced to be free" does not identify with the general will, but rather with his own private will. And from that perspective, he refuses to distinguish personal dependence from collective dependence.

Recall the question Rousseau seeks to answer – what can make our chains legitimate? He wants to say that chains are legitimate insofar as they bind us to the general will. But in recognizing the "absolute and naturally independent existence" of each individual, Rousseau seems to license the standpoint of the man who sees chains as chains, who sees being forced as being forced, and who insists that "being forced to be free" is just another word for slavery. The powers of society are there to protect and sustain him, but he experiences them as alien powers. Can Rousseau show this man to be mistaken?

Rousseau admits that in entering the civil state, one loses "his natural freedom and an unlimited right to everything that tempts him and that he can get." (CVW4.141, OC3.364) This is the liberty of the "absolute and naturally independent" individual. In its place, one gains "civil freedom and the proprietorship of everything he possesses" and "moral freedom, which alone makes man truly the master of himself." (CW4.141–2, OC3.364–5) Moral freedom replaces the slavery of appetite with the freedom of obedience "to the law one has prescribed for oneself." (CW4.142, OC3.365) But what sort of freedom or liberty is this? Rousseau claims that "[t]his passage from the state of nature to the civil state produces a remarkable change in man, by substituting justice for instinct in his behavior and giving his actions the morality they previously lacked. . . . the voice of duty replaces physical impulse and right replaces appetite." (CW4.141, OC3.364) In the state of nature each individual has only his own desires as a basis for action. Without a standard for judging these desires, he is their slave rather than their master. He has no real will of his own. But in the civil state, an individual has at least the opportunity to identify with a will that rests on interests that he shares with his fellows, thereby providing him with a standard for judging his own desires. His perfectibility enables him to transcend the limitations of his individual self, to identify with others, and to act on a basis that he shares with them. In so doing, he becomes the master of his desires. To be sure, in totally alienating himself to the body politic, he externalizes his natural sentiment of existence. But in receiving himself, together with his fellows, as an indivisible part of this same body, he reinternalizes that sentiment. In recognizing that his very existence depends on the republic, he does not think himself dependent on what is alien to him, but dependent rather on what he most truly is – the city of which he is citizen. He finds himself able to act, not without regard to his needs and desires, but on the basis of laws that recognize those needs and desires as on a par with those of his fellows. To say, as Rousseau does in *Emile*, that the citizen is raised "for others" is then misleading and indeed strictly incorrect. For the citizen is not raised to ignore himself, nor to serve those whom he experiences as other; the citizen is raised to serve the collective whole that incorporates his interests, that demands his participation, and with which he identifies himself. The citizen is raised for the greater self that he finds in society.

But even if this is Rousseau's meaning, his account in Book I of the *Social Contract* does not resolve the paradox of being "forced to be free," because it admits the "absolute and independent existence" of each individual. And from this standpoint, the general will is an alien will; the powers of society are alien powers. "Moral freedom" is no more than a change of masters – from the rule of desire to the rule of the other. Elsewhere, Rousseau tells a somewhat different story, introducing the political counterpart of the Tutor. "The general will is always right, but the judgment that guides it is not always enlightened. It must be made to see objects as they are, or sometimes as they should appear to be. . . . From this arises the necessity for a legislator." (CW4.154, OC3.380)

Who is the Legislator? Rousseau is not speaking here of the sovereign, who *enacts* the law, but rather of the person who makes the "discovery of the best rules of society suited to Nations" and gives or proposes them as laws for the sovereign to enact. He must be "a superior intelligence, who saw all of men's passions yet experienced none of them; who had no relationship at all to our nature yet knew it thoroughly; whose happiness was independent of us, yet who was nevertheless willing to attend to ours." (CW4.154, OC3.381) He "is an extraordinary man in the State in all respects. . . . This function, which constitutes the republic, does not enter into its constitution. It is a particular and superior activity that has nothing in common with human dominion." (CW4.155, OC3.382) In effect, the Legislator stands outside the society whose general will he guides. Just as the Tutor must understand what it is to be a natural man in a world in which men have lost their original nature, so the Legislator must understand what it is to be a citizen in a world in which there are only masters and slaves. Rousseau never explains how either can exist.

This is a serious problem. But I shall let Rousseau believe that he can answer it, and turn to his account of the Legislator's task.

One who dares to undertake the founding of a people should feel that he is capable of changing human nature, so to speak; of transforming each individual, who by himself is a perfect and solitary whole, into a part of a larger whole from which this individual receives, in a sense, his life and his being; of altering man's constitution in order to strengthen it; of substituting a partial and moral existence for the physical and independent existence we have all received from nature. He must, in short, take away man's own forces in order to give him forces that are foreign to him and that he cannot make use of without the help of others. The more these natural forces are dead and destroyed, and the acquired ones great and lasting, the more the institution as well is solid and perfect. So that if each Citizen is nothing, and can do nothing, except with all the others, and if the force acquired by the whole is equal or superior to the sum of the natural forces of all the individuals, it may be said that legislation has reached its highest possible point of perfection. (CW4.155, OC3.381–2)

Note the emphasis on "the help of others," and on being and doing "nothing except with all the others." The task of the Legislator is to extinguish the absolute and independent existence of each individual, and to replace it with a relative, partial, and dependent existence – dependent, of course, on the collective body of the community of which one is part. In this way, the Legislator creates the citizen. The true *force* that makes one free is what makes one a citizen. It is not the force that constrains one to obey the general will in the face of one's private interests, but rather the force that denatures one, takes away one's original sentiment of existence in oneself, which is the ground of private interest, and replaces it with the sentiment of existence as a member of the community, which is the ground of public interest and the general will. The force that makes one free takes away one's dependence on the private wills of others, and the need to speak the enslaving words, *aidez-moi*. In their place, it makes one dependent on the community with which it leads one to identify oneself, and gives one the opportunity to speak the liberating words of mutual assistance, *aidons-nous*.

The denaturing of the citizen appears quite explicitly in Émile, when Rousseau distinguishes him from the natural man.

Natural man is entirely for himself. He is numerical unity, the absolute whole which is relative only to itself or its kind. Civil man is only a fractional unity dependent on the denominator; his value is determined by his relation to . . . the social body. Good social institutions are those that best know how to denature man, to take his absolute existence from him in order to give him a relative one and transport the *I* into the common unity, with the result that each individual believes himself no longer one but a part of the unity and no longer feels except within the whole. (Bl.39–40, OC4.249)

Rousseau believed that this denaturing was realized in republican Rome, where a citizen "was neither Caius nor Lucius; he was a Roman. He even loved the country [*patrie*] exclusive of himself." (Bl.40, OC4.249)

Love of the country, "*la patrie*," is the core emotion of the citizen. In the *Discourse on Political Economy*, Rousseau represents this love, *amour de la patrie* as a transformation of the *amour propre* that leads each person to demand to be foremost. Each citizen must believe and demand that his country be foremost. In this way, Rousseau claims, we "transform into a sublime virtue this dangerous disposition from which all our vices rise." (CW3.155, OC3.260) For "[i]t is certain that the greatest miracles of virtue have been produced by love of fatherland [*amour de la patrie*]. By combining the force of amour propre with all the beauty of virtue, this sweet and ardent feeling gains an energy which . . . makes it the most heroic of all the passions." (CW3.151, OC3.255)

The *Discourse on Political Economy* offers Rousseau's most extended account of the transformative education of the citizen. Education is the key task of the government, emphasized by the ancients but ignored and forgotten by the moderns. Rousseau acknowledges the necessity of establishing peace and order, but insists that the government that limits itself to seeking obedience will find difficulty in being obeyed. "If it is good to know how to use men as they are, it is better still to make them what one needs them to be. The most absolute authority is that which penetrates to the inner man and is exerted no less on his will than on his actions." (CW3.148, OC3.251) Perfect subjection, as the Tutor has insisted, makes the will captive. (Bl.120, OC4.362) How is this achieved; how does one make citizens as society needs them? "Now, forming citizens is not accomplished in a day, and to have them as men they must be taught as children. . . . If . . . they are trained early enough never to consider their persons except as related to the body of the State, and not to perceive their own existence, so to speak, except as part of the state's, they will eventually come to identify themselves in some way with this larger whole; to feel themselves to be members of the fatherland; to love it with that exquisite sentiment[2] that any isolated man feels only for himself; to elevate their soul perpetually toward this great object" (CW3.154–5, OC3.259–60), and so to transform the dangerous *amour propre* into the sublime virtue of *amour de la patrie*. "It is from the first moment of life that one must learn to deserve to live; and since one shares the rights of citizens at birth, the instant of our birth should be the beginning of the performance of our duties." (CW3.155, OC3.260) For Rousseau, duty is

---

[2] Bush tr., "delicate feeling."

inseparable from citizenship – a connection that, as we shall see later, dooms both in his eyes.

The need for a Legislator and the key importance of education reappear in Rousseau's last overtly political writing, the *Considerations on the Government of Poland*.[3] In the modern world he finds no true legislators; in the ancient world he finds Moses, Lycurgus, and Numa – lawgivers to the Jews, the Spartans, and the Romans. "The same spirit guided all ancient Lawgivers and their institutions. All of them sought bonds that might attach the Citizens to the fatherland and to one another, and they found them in distinctive practices, . . . religious ceremonies . . . , games . . . , exercises . . . , spectacles."[4] (Go.181, OC3.958) And the result is that

[u]pon opening its eyes, a child should see the fatherland, and see only it until his dying day. Every true republican drank love of fatherland, that is to say love of the laws and of freedom, with his mother's milk. This love makes up his whole existence; he sees only his fatherland, he lives only for it; when he is alone, he is nothing: when he no longer has a fatherland, he no longer is, and if he is not dead, he is worse than dead. (Go.189, OC3.966)

---

[3] Rousseau wrote this work in response to a request from the Polish Count Wielhorski, who sought advice on reforming the almost anarchic Polish government before the surrounding powers – Austria, Prussia, and Russia – had succeeded in totally dismembering the Polish state. In the event, hopes for reform came to naught and Poland soon ceased to exist as an independent polity. Rousseau's proposals were, of course, adapted to the peculiar circumstances of the country for which they were intended, but his emphasis on education and his appeal to a Legislator are fully in line with the political theory he had developed in earlier writings.

[4] Rousseau speaks in the spirit of these Legislators in his *Letter to d'Alembert*, proposing the introduction of public festivals (rather than the theater) in Geneva, as "an important component of the training in law and order and good morals" (CW10.347, OC5.119), and as a means for bringing back those citizens who have made their living abroad, by reawakening their memories: "Ah! where are the games and festivals of my youth? Where is the concord of the citizens? Where is the public fraternity? . . . Let us go and seek out all that again." (CW10.349, OC5.121)

This is the fruit of the "national education," which "is suitable only for free men; only they enjoy a common existence and are truly bound together by Law." (Ibid.)

In this last passage four important ideas are juxtaposed. First is the idea of a national education, an education for a particular political community with its unique mores. Rousseau contrasts this with the education of "[a] Frenchman, an Englishman, a Spaniard, an Italian, a Russian," who are "all more or less the same man,"[5] and who leave school "molded . . . for servitude." (Go.189, OC3.966) Second is the idea of a free man, who is the product of a national education. Freedom, Rousseau insists, requires participation in a particular community, rather than existence in an amorphous society. Third is the idea of a common existence, and Rousseau's insistence that free persons and only free persons enjoy such an existence. Indeed, we may say that freedom and identification with the particular community are one – provided, as the fourth idea makes clear, that the members of the community are bound by law, the expression of the general will that they share. National education, freedom, common existence, and law thus are the components in Rousseau's idea of the citizen, who is the product of an education binding him to his particular community, which affords him civil freedom, and in which he experiences his existence in common with his fellows under the bonds of law.

Consider again Rousseau's question: what can make our chains legitimate? We are chained to society, and we cannot loose our chains and hope to survive, whether as individuals or as a species. Rousseau offers several ways of conceptualizing our relationship to society, endeavoring to show that its chains are legitimate. I have distinguished three ideas: alienation, participation, identification. Each individual voluntarily alienates himself to society in the act of agreement, the social compact, by which it is

[5] A claim that would surely have astonished these persons.

formed. Each citizen participates as a member of the sovereign, the ruling, law-making body of society. And each citizen perceives his own existence only as part of society and so identifies himself with the society. Although he does not discuss the relationship among these three ideas in detail, Rousseau would, I think, want to insist that the first two are necessary to the third. But this may be misleading. For if each citizen is raised truly to identify with his society, so that he perceives his existence only as a part of it, then he will lack any sense of an independent self that must be alienated, or of a private interest that must be brought into harmony with his fellows. His participation in sovereignty will be simply an expression of his solidarity with the collective body. There will be no one with a particular will who must be "forced to be free." "Good social institutions are those that best know how to denature man." (Bl.40, OC4.249) The citizen knows nothing of the free individual, who "wants only what he can do and does what he pleases." (Bl.84, OC4.309) Instead, he wants only what his society, his *patrie*, can do, and does what pleases it. This is the true freedom of the citizen. The balance of needs and powers lost in the passage from solitude to society is restored by identifying both one's needs and one's powers with those of one's *patrie*.

The words *aidez-moi* cannot be unspoken. There is no way back to the original condition of individual self-sufficiency in which words were unnecessary. What Rousseau proposes is that we transform *aidez-moi*, in which self and other are explicitly distinguished and the self acknowledges its dependence on the other, so that it becomes *aidons-nous*, in which self and other are united in a single whole that acknowledges only its dependence on itself and senses its existence as one. In this transformation the self, conceived initially as the independent, self-sufficient unit, is entirely annulled, and yet preserved as an inseparable part of the whole, the *nous* that can be *nous* only through including the *moi*. As the rupture between self and other is closed, *amour propre*, which presupposes that rupture, becomes *amour de la patrie*, love of the whole with which the self identifies and in which it senses its existence. The self acquires a collective and, as Rousseau insists, moral existence, insofar as it shares in the general will coming from all, and so expressing their liberty, and applying to all, and so expressing their duty in the form of submission to law. Each is subject to the law, but each is also part of the law-making sovereign, and it is this role and right that Rousseau captures in his idea of the citizen.

I have quoted at some length and from different works, so that we are in no doubt about the making of the citizen. As Rousseau says, it is not the business of a single day, since it is a process of deep and radical transformation. The individual loses his own powers, those that he can use, independently of others, to effect his own will. The individual loses his sense of independent identity, of existing as a separate self. In return, he gains access to powers that he can use only in common with his fellows, collectively, to effect their shared will. And he gains a sense of collective identity, of existing as and only as a part of a community. One might regard this transformation as enslavement, as the reduction of a naturally free individual to a mere cog in the social machine. The work of the Legislator might seem to be the creation of a dystopia comparable to *Brave New World* or *Nineteen Eighty-Four*. But as I have insisted, Rousseau's clear and overt intention is to present this transformation as liberation, as becoming a free citizen obeying only oneself.

I shall of course ask whether he successfully carries out this intention. But we should note here that whether or not he succeeds, the education of the citizen is as much an exercise in control as the education of Émile. The aim is of course very different – to create total dependence rather than to prevent it, to bring about identification with society rather than separation from it. Although both Legislator and Tutor exercise control, their roles are in fact opposed. The Tutor must prevent the denaturing of the individual; the Legislator, rather, must complete that denaturing, obliterating the fallen individual in order to create the redeemed citizen. And not only are the roles of Tutor and Legislator opposed, they are exercised in very different manners. Neither may appear to exercise the control he does. But the Tutor must act only through things, making his rule appear as the course of nature. The Legislator rules through opinions, making his rule appear as the will of the gods. He is "unable to use either force or reasoning, . . . [and so must] have recourse to the intervention of heaven." (CW4.156, OC3.383) Neither Émile nor the citizen understands the true basis of his supposed freedom.

We have seen who the citizen is and how he is made. How does Rousseau relate his ideal of citizenship to himself as Citizen of Geneva? Before we can answer this question, we must consider how the ideal relates to Rousseau's understanding of citizenship in Geneva. In the sixth of the *Letters Written from the Mountain*, Rousseau summarizes the argument of the *Social Contract*. The letters are a response to the *Letters Written from the Country*, published anonymously but known to be from the pen of Jean-Robert Tronchin, procurer-general of Geneva and leader of the successful movement to burn Rousseau's writings and to order his arrest. This was not a gratuitous attack on Rousseau, but reflected the division of Geneva between the citizens and bourgeois who were all members of the nominally sovereign General Council, and the wealthy magistrates and religious leaders who dominated the Little Council, the directive body of the state, and the consultative Council of Two Hundred. By electing each other, these oligarchic bodies were self-perpetuating. Tronchin recognized the import of Rousseau's theories for Genevan politics, and he moved decisively to block their influence. The two sets of letters thus embody the fundamentally opposed views of the Genevan polity held on the one hand by the activists among the bourgeois citizenry and, on the other, by the patrician magistracy. But my concern is not to pursue the history of this controversy, but rather to examine the connection, as Rousseau saw it, between the ideal political order of the *Social Contract* and the actual political order of Geneva.

After summarizing the *Social Contract*, Rousseau addresses his imaginary reader, a Genevan bourgeois who has not committed himself to either side of the controversy. "What do you think, Sir, upon reading this short and faithful analysis of my Book? I guess it. You are saying to yourself; there is the history of the Government of Geneva. That is what all those who are acquainted with your Constitution say upon reading the same Work." (CW9.233, OC3.809) So for Rousseau, the citizen who unites with his fellows in exercising the general will, seeing himself as an indivisible part of the social whole, is not only an ideal, but also real, embodied as the citizen of Geneva.

Now this connection, between ideal citizen and citizen of Geneva, is of the first importance for grasping the movement of Rousseau's political thought. The *Discourse on the Origin of Inequality* reveals the wretchedness of the social bondage in which modern humans find themselves. But the bonds, alienating as they are, can be transformed into legitimate ties; this is the message of the *Social Contract*. Rousseau then reveals that these legitimate ties are already to be found in his own country, in Geneva. But if we then turn back to the *Discourse on Inequality*, and read now, not its official text, but the Epistle Dedicatory, we shall find that this is no new revelation. For the Epistle already contains the account of Geneva that, for Rousseau, makes it the embodiment of the redeeming society.

The Epistle is addressed "[t]o[6] the Republic of Geneva: Magnificent, Most Honored, and Sovereign Lords." (CW3.3, OC3.111) It offers the *Discourse on Inequality* as the fruit of thirty years' labor "to deserve to offer you public homage." (Ibid.) Thirty years would take Rousseau back just before his twelfth birthday, and about four years before he left Geneva and abjured

---

[6] Bush tr. omits "to."

the Protestant faith of his compatriots. But let us not cavil. In a series of apostrophes, Rousseau identifies the happy features that unite him to Geneva, making it his birthplace of choice. He has become the Citizen, and so he substitutes, for his real birth, and the real life in which Geneva played a secondary role, his chosen birth as Citizen, for which Geneva is central. In the apostrophes, we read the self-construction of Rousseau as Citizen of Geneva.

"I would have chosen," he tells us, "a society of a size limited by the extent of human faculties" (CW3.3, OC3.111), "a country where the Sovereign and the people could have only one and the same interest." (CW3.4, OC3.112) "I would have wished to live and die free, that is to say so subject to the laws that neither I nor anyone else could shake off their honorable yoke." (Ibid.) "I would therefore have wished that no one in the State could declare himself above the law." (Ibid.) "I would not have wished to live in a newly instituted Republic, however good its laws might be." (Ibid.) "I would have wished to choose for myself a Fatherland diverted by its fortunate impotence from the fierce love of Conquests." (CW3.5, OC3.113) "I would have sought a Country where the right of legislation was common to all Citizens," but "I would have desired that . . . everyone did not have the power to propose new Laws according to his fancy; that this right belonged exclusively to the Magistrates." (CW3.5, OC3.113–14) "Above all I would have fled, as necessarily ill-governed, a Republic where the People . . . would imprudently have retained the administration of Civil affairs and the execution of its own Laws." (CW3.6, OC3.114) "Rather I would have chosen that Republic where the individuals, being content to give sanction to the Laws and to decide in a Body and upon the report of their Chiefs the most important public affairs, would establish respected tribunals, . . . [and] elect from year to year the most capable and most upright of their Fellow Citizens to administer Justice and govern the State." (Ibid.)

These features, which Rousseau "would have chosen," are of course ascribed to Geneva. And they include the central tenet of his political theory, that "the right of legislation was common to all Citizens." But note how circumscribed this right is. For it does not include the right of initiation, which is reserved to the body of magistrates. In Genevan terms, the General Council of the bourgeois citizenry has the right to legislate; the Little Council of patricians has the right to initiate. Furthermore, in accordance with Rousseau's insistence on dividing the legislative power from administration, executive power is also in the hands of the Little Council. So the exercise of sovereign power, the determination of the general will, comes to no more than the right of the citizens, assembled in General Council, to grant, and so also to refuse, their approval to the proposed laws put before them. And it is just this right that is to bind them into a single body.

We should note one important fact about the Genevan citizenry that Rousseau seems not to find any need to mention. We must not assume that the body of citizens included all of the adult inhabitants, or adult male inhabitants, or even adult male native inhabitants, of Geneva. Even among this last group, the citizenry was a minority. Geneva was a republic, but not in our terms a democracy. In the verse epistle he wrote some years previously to the Lyonnais surgeon Parisot, Rousseau spoke of the "cruel good" of freedom he possessed, "having by my birth / the right to participate in the supreme power / Small as I was, weak obscure Citizen / I was however member of the sovereign." (OC2.1137, my trans.) Citizenship was a birthright, but birth was not sufficient for the right. Rousseau was privileged. He does not think to defend his privilege, or to explain how those native to Geneva but not among its citizens, might be free – any more than he explains how women might be free. These are important concerns, and they reveal a lack of inclusiveness in Rousseau's doctrine of the citizen, but my concern is not primarily with the scope of citizenship. Rather, I want to consider how Rousseau was influenced by his view of the rights of the citizens of Geneva, and what this reveals about his ideal of the citizen.

The *Epistle to Parisot* continues with the very un-Rousseauean claim that "I renounced forever these fierce maxims / bitter and early fruits of native prejudice / which since early years by their pungent leaven / have nourished the pride of republican hearts: . . . / It would not be good in society / that there be less inequality between the ranks." (OC2.1140, my trans.) These words came before the illumination on the road to Vincennes. They show that Rousseau's conception of republican sovereignty – the idea that each citizen participates in the supreme power and is thereby free – preceded his endorsement of it. The voice of the *Epistle to Parisot* is that of a younger Rousseau, one who recognized republican freedom without yet valuing it – hence his characterization of it as a "cruel good." And the voice reveals to us that when Rousseau came, as a result of his illumination, to seek a politics that would legitimize the chains we cannot loose, he took his inspiration from his own Genevan citizenship – or rather, the citizenship that was his before his conversion to Catholicism. Participation in sovereignty provided him with the transformative link in the chains of society, uniting the individual with the collective body so that the *aidez-moi* that each of us must speak becomes the *aidons-nous* that we speak together.

But if Rousseau's ideal of citizenship was modeled on what he took to be the constitution of Geneva, he was not unaware of the extent to which the struggle between bourgeois and patricians had led to the concentration of effective power in the hands of the latter, exercised by the Little Council. As I have noted, Rousseau understood the sovereignty of the General Council to extend to the right to approve or reject the proposals put to it. But if this right is to be effective, then the General Council must be the guardian of the law. Otherwise, as Rousseau argued, the General Council would be saying to the Little Council, "Gentlemen, behold the Body of Laws that we establish in the State, and of which we make you the depositories, in order for you to conform to it when you judge it appropriate, and in order to transgress it when you please." (CW9.265, OC3.847, italicized in original)

Rousseau thus established a fundamental distinction between the right to enact law, and the right to preserve what had been enacted. In an attempt to resolve the disputes between the conflicting parties in Geneva, the citizens had been given the right of representation – the right to put their concerns before the Little Council. Rousseau saw this right as having two parts. On the one hand, the citizens had the right to suggest changes in the law – but such proposals were for the consideration of the Little Council, which had no obligation to submit them to the General Council for ratification or rejection. On the other hand, the citizens had the right to protest violations of the existing law – and such protests could not be dismissed by the Little Council, but rather had to be submitted to the General Council for determination. This understanding of the right of representation was denied by the Little Council, which insisted that the right of representation left the Little Council free to dispose, whether of a proposal or a protest, without bringing it to the General Council. And this, Rousseau saw, undermined the real sovereignty of the Genevan citizenry.

But even if what Rousseau believed to be the sovereign right of the citizen had been more effectively recognized, Geneva would clearly have fallen far short of his ideal. In the first place, the ongoing conflict among the citizens showed the extent to which their private wills took precedence over the general will. Indeed, if we think of the general will as residing primarily in the voice of the General Council, the members of the Little Council would have had to be "forced to be free." Recall Rousseau's vision of republican Rome, in which there was neither Caius nor Lucius, but only Romans. One could not imagine republican Geneva as composed, neither of Pierre nor of Robert, but only of Genevans.

We may of course have our doubts about Rousseau's vision of Rome, but he would hardly have been taken seriously had he offered a comparable vision of Geneva.

And in the second place, exercise of the right of representation is a poor substitute for genuine participation in sovereignty. Suppose the right had been made effective in the form that Rousseau envisaged, and even that private wills had ceased to assert themselves in opposition to the general will. Only a plebiscitary democracy would have been achieved, in which the General Council of the citizens would be invited to approve the proposals of what would be in fact, if not in name, a governing oligarchy. Geneva would not have been a genuinely participatory democracy in which each citizen entered actively into the formation of the general will. To be sure, Rousseau may never have had participatory democracy in mind in his account of sovereignty. But if each Genevan is to identify himself primarily as a citizen, as a member of the body politic, then surely he must find himself actively engaged in the determination of its general will. Rousseau's radical conception of citizenship as constituting the primary identity of the members of society clearly requires an equally radical conception of the citizen's role. In failing to recognize this, Rousseau created a gap between his political theory and his analysis of actual political societies.

Rousseau called himself Citizen of Geneva, but we cannot imagine him being not Jean-Jacques but simply a Genevan. I shall claim that he knew, in himself, that the alleged freedom of the ideal citizen was a false freedom. But we shall need his autobiographical self-understanding to draw that conclusion. Here I want to turn, as in the previous chapter, to the *Dialogues*, and their deconstructive message. My focus is on Rousseau's implicit understanding of his fundamental legitimating device, the general will.

Recall that the role of the Legislator is to ensure that "each Citizen is nothing, and can do nothing, except with all the others."

Different as this role is from that of the Tutor who must rather ensure that Émile can do everything without the aid of others, it also has its reflection in the acts of the nameless "gentlemen" who, in Rousseau's paranoid vision in the *Dialogues*, rule the destiny of the hapless Jean-Jacques. For they deprive him of the use of his own powers to satisfy his desires: "simply showing the desire for anything whatsoever is for him the infallible method of making it disappear." (CW1.42, OC1.713) But new powers are provided, so that "in preventing him from following his wishes and accomplishing his evil designs, they still seek to obtain the sweet things of life for him, so that he finds what he needs everywhere." (CW1.44, OC1.716) And so "they publicly offer him alms despite himself in such a way that he cannot avoid them." (CW1.46, OC1.718) Reduced to nothing in himself, Jean-Jacques is nevertheless sustained by the powers of the whole that controls him.

This places Jean-Jacques in a quite extraordinary position. In the Second Promenade of the *Reveries*, Rousseau, referring to the supposed universal plot against him, insists that "this universal agreement is too extraordinary to be purely fortuitous. If there had been a single man who had refused to be an accomplice to it, . . . that would have been enough to make it fail. But all the acts of will . . . have made firm the work of men." (CW8.15, OC1.1010) The plot is thus founded on a will that is general, in being shared by all members of society – save, it seems, Jean-Jacques himself. Instead, he is the primary *object* of that will. In a remarkable passage in the *Dialogues*, the character Rousseau says: "While he [Jean-Jacques] is occupied with himself, they are occupied with him too. He loves himself and they hate him. . . . He is everything to himself; he is also everything to them. For as for them, they are nothing[7] either to him or to themselves; and as long as J. J. is miserable, they need no

---

[7] Recall Rousseau's use of this same phrase to describe the final condition of extreme inequality in the *Discourse on Inequality*.

other happiness." (CW1.154–5, OC1.860) Each person, nothing in himself, has come to live through, and only through, his awareness of Jean-Jacques' misery; his existence is externalized in the universal conspiracy.

But is not Jean-Jacques himself alien to the society whose existence consists in execrating him? If so, this prevents us from identifying the will expressed in the universal plot as in any sense a general will, since a general will must both come from all and *apply* equally to all. The general will, Rousseau insists, is always right but "loses its natural rectitude when it is directed toward any individual, determinate object." (CW4.149, OC3.373) It creates a universal dependence, but precisely in order to exclude any particular dependence. The will of the universal plot, by contrast, is directed at Jean-Jacques, making him dependent.

Recall, however, that "each individual can, as a man, have a private will contrary to or differing from the general will he has as a Citizen." (CW4.140–1, OC3.363) And the person who, acting on his private will, disobeys the general will is destructive to society and, Rousseau claims, to himself. He has already told us that such a person must be "forced to be free." This is precisely the situation of Jean-Jacques – the Citizen who is forced to be free. Rousseau in the *Dialogues* reports him as asking, "Ah, Sir, can't you see that the great, the only crime they fear from me, a horrible crime the fear of which keeps them in continuous dread, is my justification?" (CW1.140, OC1.841) Jean-Jacques' crime, making him "the horror of the human race" (CW1.36, OC1.705), is his refusal to admit his guilt, his persistence in justifying himself. For this justification, placing him in opposition to society, is an affirmation of his private will against what the society claims to be the general will. Hence he is proscribed by "a unanimous agreement" (CW8.3, OC1.995) in which society seeks to force him to participate.

It may seem that by appealing to the right of society to force its members to be free, we can reconcile this unanimous accord with the doctrine of the general will. In order to do this, we should have to recognize that this accord is not itself an act of the general will, since it is not an act of legislation. But legislation must be applied to particular cases, which is the task of government or magistracy.[8] Hence it may seem that we should think of the universal proscription as the way in which the citizens, acting as magistrates, apply the will of their society to the recalcitrant Jean-Jacques, and in so doing affirm their own endorsement of that will and their solidarity with each other. But what is this will? If it is a general will, what is its universal content – what does it require that Jean-Jacques is supposed to repudiate? In Rousseau's account, the will of the society that proscribes Jean-Jacques has no content beyond that proscription. Execration of him is the bond that unites the members of society, and grounds their collective will.

Jean-Jacques affirms his individuality in the face of totalitarian society, and so denies that the will of society is truly general. Faced with his challenge, the society must seek to respond by requiring him to confess, thus withdrawing his assertion of individual will in favor of the general will. But this still leaves the occurrence of the act of assertion as a fact. And so the society must respond by making the individual a nonperson, a person who does not exist, who never existed, so that no opposed assertion of individual will has ever occurred. Remarkably, Rousseau, like George Orwell in *Nineteen Eighty-Four*, is aware of the totalitarian need to control the past. The Frenchman says, "The further they move into the future, the easier it is for them to obliterate the past or give it the aspect that suits them." (CW1.220–1, OC1.944) Indeed, we may

---

[8] Rousseau discusses government at length in Book III of the *Social Contract*. The key idea is that sovereignty, expressed in the general will, determines the framework within which magistracy is exercised. (v. OC3.195–7) The magistrate applies the universal principles laid down by the general will to particular situations. One such situation would be created by a (supposed) citizen who took his private will rather than the general will as determining his conduct.

interpret Rousseau's attempt to deposit the manuscript of the *Dialogues* on the great altar of Notre Dame in Paris as aimed at preserving a record of himself against "their" attempts to erase him from history. The attempt, not surprisingly, failed, but of course his paranoia would induce him to judge any attempt, once made, as a failure.

Jean-Jacques is an enemy of society, affirming his individual will, but from the standpoint of society no enemy is possible, since the general will embraces all. Because he is an enemy – indeed, *the* enemy – execrating him is an affirmation of social legitimacy that, in acknowledging the reality of his enmity and defiance, undermines that legitimacy. It purports to be the core act of the general will, affording not only happiness but existence to the members of society, but it denies its status as such an act by taking a particular object. Jean-Jacques is therefore the object of universal but *concealed* execration. The "gentlemen" see to it that he is never confronted or accused. For accusation would openly reveal the contradiction in the general will and admit the existence, and thereby the legitimacy, of his individuality.

In Rousseau's admittedly paranoid vision, the will of society is seen as imposed on Jean-Jacques, rather than as arising from him as an indivisible part of the whole. But before we dismiss this account as political fantasy, we should reflect on the emergence of totalitarianism in the modern world, which offers striking testimony to the power of his vision. A society in which "each Citizen is nothing, and can do nothing, except with all the others" is the antithesis of the liberating force that Rousseau seeks.

And so let Rousseau's Legislator do his work, creating a society in which each citizen is and can be nothing without the others. But let there be one flaw in the work – Jean-Jacques himself, who remains "a perfect and solitary whole." (CW4.155, OC3.381) He resists every attempt to deprive him of his self-sufficiency, to make him dependent on powers that can be exercised only collectively. If his resistance reveals a truth about human nature that the

Legislator's activity denies, then how shall his fellows, who must not know that truth, regard him – save as the scandal of the human race? And how shall he regard himself?

Rousseau thinks of himself as the Citizen of Geneva. But as our investigation of his autobiographical works will reveal more clearly, his life is a denial of all citizenship, of any attempt to force him into the dependence on his fellows that true citizenship would demand. For him, the first words of the citizen, *aidons-nous*, cannot be spoken.

4

In Julie's Garden

"I must flee you, Mademoiselle." (CW6.25, OC2.31) Thus Julie's tutor begins his first letter to his pupil of a year. The words are a declaration of love. In the more than seven hundred pages[1] that follow, we read the "Letters of Two Lovers Who Live in a Small Town at the Foot of the Alps" (CW6.1, OC2.3) – and the letters of those caught up in their story. For many of us Rousseau is the author of the *Social Contract*, the *Discourse on the Origin of Inequality*, the *Confessions*, perhaps *Emile*. But in his lifetime, and for some years thereafter, by far the most widely read of his books was his novel, *Julie*, subtitled *The New Eloise* (*La nouvelle Héloïse*). The subtitle may mislead; the lovers are indeed tutor and pupil, but their circumstances, and their fates, differ markedly from those of Eloïse and Abelard.[2] The novel, despite its length, tells a simple, unconvoluted story, which I shall recount after briefly placing *Julie* in my overall reading of Rousseau. It was published shortly before *Emile* and the *Social Contract*. All three reflect the illumination on the road to Vincennes, and the Fall portrayed in the *Discourses*. But it was conceived rather later than these other works and moves beyond them in two important respects.

---

[1] Counting by the Gallimard edition of Rousseau's works.
[2] This is one reason that, unlike most commentators, I prefer to refer to the novel as *Julie*.

Julie contains its own redemptive vision, but it also contains its own deconstruction of that vision, not leaving the task to be performed implicitly and elsewhere. And that deconstruction leads to another, deeper vision, not present in *Emile* or the *Social Contract*. For the agent of deconstruction, appropriately to the story, is love – the love between Julie and her tutor. As we shall see, the novelistic significance of love, as we might call it, is clear, but its philosophic significance, as it figures in *Julie*, is only suggested. To understand that, we must await Rousseau's autobiographical self-construction, in which love appears at the center of his last redemptive vision, its presence filling that final promenade that, as I noted at the outset, is the object of my enquiries. *Julie*, on my reading, is a pivotal work; it is the forerunner of the shift from concern with *aidez-moi* to concern with *aimez-moi* that provides the positive dynamic of Rousseau's thought.

Let us then turn to the story. A young man of humble origins, whose name we never know, but who later is given the alias St. Preux, is tutor to two slightly younger women of noble birth, Julie and Claire, cousins and inseparable friends. In the first letter, as I have said, the tutor declares his love to Julie, which, after an appropriate delay, she confesses to reciprocate. Many of the ensuing details need not concern us, but we need to know of her father's implacable unwillingness to let her wed a man of lowly origins, and his determination instead that she marry a friend he has made, a man of aristocratic but not fully revealed background, much older than Julie, M. de Wolmar. We need also to know that the love of Julie and her tutor is consummated, twice, the second occasion resulting in her pregnancy, terminated unwittingly when Julie's father, enraged by Julie's love but unaware of her condition, beats her mercilessly. And we need to know of another person, a wealthy English peer, Milord Edward Bomston, who befriends the tutor and proposes to no avail to bestow up to half his fortune on the young man, if Julie's father will but consent to the marriage of the lovers.

The tutor, heartsick, is forced to leave his post, but continues correspondence with his beloved until his letters are discovered. He then reluctantly renounces the right she had given him, to give his consent before she would marry. Obedient to her father, she marries M. de Wolmar, and finds, or claims to find, herself changed and indeed transformed, as she recognizes the need to sacrifice her heart's desires to the law of duty. While vowing unending friendship, she breaks off all direct relations with her former lover. Five years have elapsed since his first declaration of love.

Almost six more years pass before our story resumes, more than three of them spent at sea by the former tutor. Returned, he is invited by M. de Wolmar, who knows of his wife's past attachment to him, to the estate at Clarens where Wolmar, Julie, their two children, and her father live. Wolmar, a man without passion whose life is spent in the observation of his fellows, has developed, with Julie, an apparently ideal and idyllic community, and now intends to bring together all those who are united by bonds of friendship – the inseparable Claire, who had also married but is now widowed; her daughter, who is already resident at Clarens; Julie's former lover and tutor, now called St. Preux; and Milord Edward Bomston. Bomston, however, is occupied with his own amours in Rome, and in letters to him the tutor writes at length about the political economy of the estate, and about Julie's own retreat, the garden that is her Elysium. As we shall see, both of these discussions shed light on Rousseau's redemptive concern.

Wolmar tests the former lovers by arranging to leave them together while he is absent on business, and tests St. Preux further by observing his attitude to Julie's father, who had of course forbidden his relationship with Julie. Satisfied that love has given way to the deepest friendship, he proposes to make St. Preux the children's tutor. Julie, meanwhile, encourages St. Preux and Claire to marry, a suggestion neither accepts. But first St. Preux is called away by Bomston, who needs his help and advice in putting an end to his amours.

And so we are ready for the dénouement. One of Julie's children falls into the lake; she jumps in to save him. He is rescued, but the strain on her system is too great, and she contracts a fatal fever. Dying, she writes St. Preux a last letter, which Wolmar encloses with a long account of her illness and death. "We must abandon our plans. . . . We were planning to reunite: this reunion was not good. . . . For a long time I have lived an illusion.[3] This illusion[4] for me was salutary; it collapses at the moment when I no longer need it." (CW6.608, OC2.740) I pass to the final paragraph:

Farewell, farewell my sweet friend. . . . Alas! I end my life as I began it. I say too much, perhaps, at this moment when the heart no longer dissembles anything.[5] . . . Ah why should I shrink from expressing all that I feel? It is no longer I who speak to you [and here Julie passes from the formal '*vous*' with which she has long addressed her erstwhile lover to the intimate '*tu*'];[6] I am already in death's embrace. When you see this letter, worms will gnaw your lover's face, and her heart where you shall reside no more.[7] But would my soul exist without you, without you what felicity should I enjoy? No, I am not leaving you[8], I go to await you. The virtue that separated us on earth shall unite us in the eternal abode. I

---

3 Stewart and Vaché tr., "I have long deluded myself"; Fr. "*Je me suis longtems fait illusion.*" Further notes omit translators' names.
4 Tr., "delusion"; Fr. "*illusion.*"
5 Tr., "a thing"; Fr. "*rien.*"
6 Trans. uses "thee," "thou," "thy," and appropriate verb forms in the remainder. There is (as the translators recognize) in fact no satisfactory way to express this shift in English. In the first place, Julie and her lover have passed from the formal to the informal and vice versa at several points in the early part of the novel. The French reader will be aware of this; the English reader will not. And in the second place, the shift to the intimate "tu" gives the French reader final proof of Julie's true feelings, whereas the use of "thou" unavoidably gives the contemporary English reader a sense of artificiality that is the very antithesis of the intended intimacy.
7 Tr., "no longer dwell"; Fr. "*ne seras plus.*"
8 Tr., "Nay, I leave thee not"; Fr. "*Non, je ne te quitte pas.*"

die in this sweet[9] expectation. Only too happy to purchase at the price of my life[10] the right to love you forever[11] without crime, and to say it to you[12] one more time. (CW6.610, OC2.743)

A final letter from Claire to St. Preux, urging him to hasten the day when he rejoins the household at Clarens, yet foretelling that the time is not far off when she herself will rejoin Julie in another realm, brings our story to its formal end. But it is Julie's dying words of undying love that – in addition no doubt to bringing out the handkerchiefs in a thousand sitting rooms and bedrooms – bring out the deep message of the book, revealing its implications for Rousseau's system of thought. That, however, is my destination in this chapter. In order to return to the ending we need to proceed through several matters, beginning with the nameless lover. I shall then consider the role of Wolmar, who, like the Tutor in *Emile* and the Legislator, appears as one of Rousseau's redemptive artificers, and the organization of the estate at Clarens, for the light it adds to my account of Rousseau's politics in the preceding chapter. Then I shall look at Julie's Elysium, the garden that reveals Rousseau's understanding of the relation between man and nature, and implicitly suggests much more. In revealing an important dimension of the relationship between Julie and her lover, it will lead me to seek to understand the idea of love that Rousseau offers in the novel,[13] and then to turn to the dénouement, to the triumph of love over artifice and to the meaning of our first words, the *aimez-moi* that, as we saw in the first chapter, Rousseau hears at the origins of the southern languages.

Julie's lover never appears under his own name. St. Preux, as I have remarked, is an alias, used only after his role of lover

9 Tr., "flattering"; Fr. "*douce.*"
10 Tr., "to pay with my life"; Fr. "*d'acheter au prix de ma vie.*"
11 Tr., "still"; Fr. "*toujours.*"
12 Tr., "tell thee so"; Fr. "*de te le dire.*"
13 And which differs from the Tutor's idea of love in *Emile*.

has apparently ended. We cannot doubt that the lover is, indeed, Jean-Jacques, although Rousseau's official role in the novel is that of editor. In the alleged conversation with a "man of letters" that makes up the long Second Preface to the book, Rousseau neither admits nor denies that he is its author, although he insists that it be read as letters in which "[t]wo or three[14] simple but sensitive[15] youths discuss among themselves the interests of their hearts." (CW6.11, OC2.16) Both the namelessness of the lover, and the ambiguous status of Rousseau as editor, are, I think, exercises in the complex pattern of identification and concealment that, as we shall see, will run through Rousseau's autobiographical works and culminate in the "Citizen of Geneva." Both provide roles in which Rousseau is able to accomplish, whether in reality as editor, or in imagination as lover, what his real self would deny him. But both also show Rousseau's uncertainty about that real self. I shall try to defend these claims in subsequent chapters, and argue that it is only at the end of his life that Rousseau is finally able to say who he is.

Although in a longer enquiry we could find much to detain us in the early parts of *Julie*, here I must focus attention primarily on aspects of its second half. The lover has returned from the sea, and is at Clarens, in the household established by Wolmar and Julie. He is there at Wolmar's behest. Why? We need to understand the nature of this unusual man. He is an unbeliever, sagacious, equable, grave, with "a tranquil soul and a cold heart." (CW6.402, OC2.490) In the last letter that she writes to her erstwhile lover after her marriage and before his long departure, Julie says, "Monsieur de Wolmar's greatest predilection is for

---

[14] The indefinite "two or three" leaves room for, without positively including, the inseparable cousin Claire, whose heart is more involved than my brief retelling of the story has been able to accommodate.

[15] Tr., "sensible." One of the referees noted that this is not the appropriate rendition of the Fr. "*sensible.*"

observation." (CW6.305, OC2.370) Later, in a letter to Claire, Julie quotes him as saying about himself,

> If I have any ruling passion it is that of observation. I like to read what is in men's hearts. . . . I scarcely err in my judgments; and that is the whole compensation for *amour propre*[16] in my continual studies; for I do not like playing a role, but only seeing others perform. I enjoy observing society, not taking part in it. If I could change the nature of my being and become a living eye, I would gladly make that exchange. Thus my indifference for men does not make me independent of them; though I care not about being seen, I need to see them." (CW6.403, OC2.491)

Amour propre is, we have seen, the comparative self-love that, unchecked, leads us to find the sense of our existence in the opinion of others rather than in ourselves. In needing to see, though not to be seen, Wolmar's existence, uniquely, is neither alienated in others nor present in himself, but finds itself in his own sense of others. He says neither "Help me!" nor "Love me!"; indeed, he has no need to say anything. His dependence on his fellows does not make him dependent on their wills, for short of becoming invisible they can deny him nothing he seeks. And so he is free. If he were a pure eye, then his freedom would be that not of an agent but of an observer. But he recognizes that this would be impossible for a man. He tells Julie, "we see nothing if we do nothing but look. . . . we must act ourselves to see men act, and I made of myself an actor in order to be a spectator." (CW6.403, OC2.492)

Wolmar also tells Julie that "[m]y only active principle is a natural taste for order." (CW6.403, OC2.490) Indeed, she had already recognized his concern with order in her first description of him:

> The order he has brought into his house is the image of the one that prevails in his heart, and seems to imitate in a small household the order established in the governance of the earth. . . . The master's hand can

---

[16] Tr., "self-love."

always be recognized and is never felt; he has so well ordained the original arrangement of things that now it runs all by itself, and discipline and freedom are enjoyed at the same time. (CW6.305–6, OC2.371–2)

✳ As God has ordered the world so that it runs without his intervention, so the demigod, Wolmar, has ordered his part of the world, his household. We should be reminded of the Tutor, who orders the life and the soul of his pupil. Substitute "Émile" for "his house," "an individual person" for "a small household," and "tutor" for "master" in the passage just quoted, and we have an exact description of what Rousseau intends the Tutor to accomplish. But even more, we should be reminded of the Legislator, and I shall pursue this parallel in examining Wolmar's work.

If Wolmar is to order his world, then he must order the souls of its inhabitants, as the Tutor seeks to order the soul of Émile. But whereas the Tutor begins with a blank slate, Wolmar encounters the disorder that has been created by the love between Julie and her tutor, a love and a disorder that have not vanished in the ending of contact or correspondence between them. It is only if each can come to know the other as friend that each can cease to sense the other as lover. Julie has said, of herself and Wolmar, "it seems we are destined to constitute but a single soul between us, of which he is the intellect and I the will." (CW6.307, OC2.374) The single soul, in which self and other merge, is, as we shall find later, Rousseau's true image of love. But until Julie can be with her former tutor and lover, and find friendship with him, she cannot know that (or if) she is, truly, one with Wolmar.[17] As for her former tutor, Wolmar seems to understand well how to integrate him into his household. He must be tutor once again, but now to Julie's children.

And so Wolmar invites his wife's former tutor and lover, now known among them as St. Preux, to join them in their model

---

[17] And of course what finally emerges is that she is one with her tutor.

estate at Clarens. What remains is for Wolmar to extend its order to embrace St. Preux, Julie's inseparable cousin Claire, and the man to whose friendship and service St. Preux has pledged himself, Milord Edward. In this community of friends, Wolmar's desire for order would be fully realized, and harmony would prevail in each person's soul, and in the relationships among them. It is, of course, not to be. But although this may appear to be the result of Julie's fatal accident, it has a deeper source. As Julie finally realizes, this harmony could not be. Yet before we pursue her realization, we need to examine Clarens, and within it, a lesser Eden within the greater, Julie's Elysium.

Our information comes from the letters that St. Preux writes from Clarens to Milord Edward, which serve both to keep us informed about the developing relationships among the principal figures, and to acquaint us with the way of life that Wolmar and Julie have established. "Everywhere they have replaced attractive things with useful things, and attractiveness has almost always come out the better. . . . Their lands are . . . farmed under their own supervision, and this farming accounts for much of their occupations, their possessions, and their pleasures." (CW6.364, OC2.442) In farming, they seek to maximize yield, not for the sake of gain, but to support a larger population – a reminder of Rousseau's claim in the *Social Contract* that increasing numbers is the surest sign of a good polity. (v. OC3.419–20) In addition to those in permanent employment, day workers are hired, with preference given to neighbors, and two prices are fixed – "the current local price, which they [Wolmar and Julie] agree to pay them for their work," and "a bonus, which they are paid only insofar as they are found satisfactory, and it almost always turns out that what they do to prove satisfactory is worth more than the extra pay they are given." (CW6.365, OC2.443) Wolmar – not always the invisible hand – checks on the laborers himself, often in the company of Julie, who at the end of the week awards a small coin to the person judged by Wolmar to have been the most diligent worker of all – "he is the intellect and I the will." St. Preux notes the appearance of expense, and the long-term reality of profit, in these measures. But not all is economics. Although Wolmar is the stern master, Julie is the benevolent mistress who shares in the pleasures, the sorrows, the lot of "all those who have served her even for a single day" and who "all become her children." (CW6.365, OC2.444)

For personal service there are eight domestics, an unusually small number for persons of their means, but calculated so that there is no opportunity for idleness. The domestics are raised to their service; St. Preux remarks, "They choose young to get them [the domestics] the way they want them." (CW6.366, OC2.444) The domestics begin at the standard wage, but yearly increments encourage them to remain. Again, apparent expense brings long-term profit. The tasks of the domestics are so arranged that "there is little communication between the two sexes: this item," St. Preux emphasizes, "is considered very important here. . . . Too intimate relations between the sexes never lead to anything but trouble." (CW6.369–70, OC2.449) Not that relations are forbidden "by explicit laws which they would be tempted to break secretly; but without any apparent intention, customs are instituted that are more powerful even than authority." (CW6.370, OC2.449) Manservants and maidservants are assigned "entirely different occupations, habits, tastes, pleasures." (CW6.370, OC2.449–50) Wolmar keeps the manservants occupied in their leisure hours with games. Here again we find the Rousseau of the political writings, emphasizing the need for the Legislator to arrange customs and practices to ensure social stability. Games play an important role in molding tastes and pleasures. Thus in the *Considerations on the Government of Poland* Rousseau asks, "How, then, can one move hearts, and get the fatherland and its laws loved? Dare I say it? with children's games; with institutions which appear trivial in the eyes of superficial men, but which form cherished habits and invincible attachments." (Go.179, OC3.955)

St. Preux, however, draws a contrast between Clarens and a true republic. He remarks, "In a Republic citizens are restrained by morals, principles, virtue: but how can domestics, mercenaries, be contained other than by constraint and coercion? The master's whole art consists in hiding this coercion under the veil of pleasure or interest, so that they think they want[18] all that they are obliged to do." (CW6.373, OC2.453) Servants are not citizens. Rousseau does not claim that Clarens embodies a general will shared alike by all its residents, both masters and servants. In a true republic, the obligations that the state lays on the citizens must express their real will. At Clarens, the obligations express what the servants "think they want." Recall the relation between pupil and tutor; "he ought to do only what he wants; but he ought to want only what you [the tutor] want him to do." (Bl.120, OC4.363) How deep is the difference here? Rousseau speaks of what the pupil wants, his alter ego St. Preux of what the domestics think they want. Now there can certainly be a difference between what one wants and what one thinks one wants; one may be mistaken in what one thinks. But no such difference seems present here; there is no suggestion that the servants are being misled into a false belief about what they want. This would be to damn arrangements that St. Preux is clearly praising. What the servants think they want is no doubt what they have been led to want, but that of course is equally true of what Émile, educated by the Tutor, wants – or what the citizens, educated in accord with the arrangements of the Legislator, want. So St. Preux assumes a genuine convergence between what the servants, properly trained, have come to want, and what they are obliged to do. Nevertheless, this convergence is not the same as that between what citizens, properly educated, have come to want and what the law

---

[18] Tr., "desire."

obliges them to do. Servants do not identify with their estate as citizens do with their state. For servants, the convergence is between personal interest and external obligation, whereas for citizens the convergence depends on identifying themselves *as* citizens so that their obligations are internalized as their interests. The question we are left with is whether this internalization can be successful. If not, then citizens are servants. And despite all he has said, St. Preux acknowledges that "[s]ervitude is so unnatural to man that it cannot possibly exist without a measure of discontent." (CW6.378, OC2.460) Even at Clarens, and even if the discontent takes the form of vying for Julie's favor.

But if the condition of servant is unnatural, the condition of peasant is not. In their relations with their neighbors, Wolmar and Julie "make a point . . . of contributing as much as they can to rendering the peasants' condition easy, without ever helping them to leave it." (CW6.438, OC2.535) A free peasant is the most self-sufficient of men, who has least need to demand "Help me!" Is there a contradiction, then, in contributing to making his condition easy? I think not, for the contribution is not a response to a demand. Insofar as it reinforces the peasant in his condition, it protects him against the *amour propre* that could lead him to seek his fortune elsewhere, in circumstances that would almost inevitably render him dependent on his fellows. St. Preux says, "Madame de Wolmar's great maxim is therefore not to favor changes of condition, but to contribute to making each one happy in his own, and above all to make sure that the happiest of all, which is that of a villager in a free State, is not depopulated in favor of the others." (CW6.439, OC2.536) In keeping the peasants in their condition, is Julie then, if not quite forcing, yet constraining them to be free?

We may observe Julie's maxim in practice, and indeed view Clarens in its fullest realization, in the last letter St. Preux writes to Milord Edward before the latter's long-delayed arrival. The theme of the letter is the grape harvest. After an initial paean to country life, coupled with the insistence that city people know and appreciate nothing of it, St. Preux turns to describe how the harvest proceeds. Each of the principals, Wolmar, Julie, Claire, and St. Preux himself, has his or her appointed supervisory role, but no more is said about this. All begin the day together with the servants and day laborers gathering grapes. This is not a fully straightforward task, since the estate makes wine of many kinds, and each requires that the grapes be gathered in a special way, imitating the effects of "twenty climates into a single one." (CW6.496, OC2.606) In the gathering, "Everyone lives in the greatest familiarity; everyone is equal, and no one forgets himself." (CW6.496, OC2.607) Thus status harmonizes with equality. "We dine with the peasants and when they do, just as we work alongside them." (Ibid.) And so the day goes.

"In the evening we all return gaily together." (CW6.497, OC2.608) Supper is served for all in the assembly hall, a plain old-fashioned room. "To avoid envy and regrets we try not to display anything to these good folks' eyes that they could not find in their own homes, to show them no opulence other than the choice of the good among common things and a little more liberality in its distribution." (CW6.498, OC2.608) The opulence – or at least what peasants if not Parisians would take for opulence – is conveniently left in the house. Status is concealed to display equality. Informality and merriment rule, and "[s]hould it happen that someone forgets himself, they [Wolmar and Julie] do not disturb the festivities with reprimands, but he is dismissed without remission the very next day." (CW6.498, OC2.609) Status bounds equality.

But supper is not the end of the day. There is still work to be done, not for the grape harvest, but in beating stalks of hemp to obtain the usable fiber. The women sing, all in chorus or by single voice and refrain, and St. Preux, very much Rousseau's mouthpiece, expresses his conviction that

> of all harmonies, there is none so agreeable as singing in unison. . . . if we need chords, it is because our taste has been depraved. Indeed, is not all harmony to be found in any sound whatsoever? And what can we add to it without distorting the proportions nature has established . . .? Nature has made everything as good as it could be; but we want to do still better, and we spoil everything.[19] (CW6.499, OC2.610)

The evening ends with a bonfire of hemp stalks, set aflame by the person, chosen by Julie, who did the most work that evening, and a drink all around.

Only at one point does melancholy intrude in this idyll – when, in the songs, phrases and expressions familiar from bygone years remind St. Preux of other times, when he and Julie hoped to be one. But he makes little of it, and we should, I think, not let a somber note distract us from the sweet melody. Rather, we should ask if the melody itself exhibits the harmony of unison. In the interplay of equality and status that I have noted, I hear, not discord, but nevertheless something other than voices all united in chorus. The peasants harvest because they must, because their livelihood requires it. The masters harvest because they will, because they choose the life that embraces it. Julie understands this difference full well in easing the peasants' condition while never helping them to leave it.

In a previous letter to Milord Edward, St. Preux makes rather strong claims about the order of Clarens.

> A small number of gentle and peaceable people, united by mutual needs and reciprocal beneficence, here work together through various tasks

---

[19] The last sentence cannot but remind us of the opening of Book I of *Emile* – "Everything is good as it leaves the hands of the Author of things; everything degenerates in the hands of men." (Bl.37, OC4.245) But note what is added – "we want to do still better." Here Rousseau indicates a direct link between perfectibility and degeneration.

toward a common goal: each one finding in his own station everything needed to be content with it and not desire to leave it, each becomes attached to it as a lifelong commitment, and his sole remaining ambition is to perform his duties well. There is such moderation in those who command and such zeal in those who obey that equals could have distributed among themselves the same functions without any one of them complaining of his lot . . . . the masters themselves gauge their happiness only by that of the people around them. (CW6.448, OC2.547–8)

Is this the picture revealed by the grape harvest? I think not. In the harvest we find the reality of status concealed behind a facade of equality. To be sure, the facade is not a mere illusion; Julie scutching the hemp is not Marie Antoinette playing at shepherdess. The masters are doing real work, and eating not cake but bread – good bread, to be sure, but shared with all. There is cake – but not for the grape harvest. The cake, and the other features of the masters' lives that cannot be shared with the others, are kept out of sight, so that they may also be out of mind – and not, as St. Preux would have it, out of mind only of those who might be aroused to envy, but also of those who do not wish to be envied. In this way, each can see himself or herself as an equal. But this is not an equality of choice. And what is not out of mind is the necessity that no one forgets himself. "Everyone lives in the greatest familiarity," as St. Preux has said, but they are, and they know they are, neither familiars nor equals. And so we might say that although Julie is a true harvester, she, and everyone else, plays at being an equal.

No one forgets himself. This is the rule of behavior, which serves to sustain the harmony of the estate. But it is also, I suggest, the rule of existence, which will serve to undermine that harmony. Wolmar can overcome the disorder created by the love of Julie and St. Preux only if he can bring them to forget themselves. But his artifice proves to extend only to the outer form of relationships, governed by rules of behavior, not to their inner being, governed by rules of existence. This will become clearer when we return to consider the dénouement of our story. But I want to point to a political as well as a personal moral. As I noted in the previous chapter, Rousseau believes, or claims to believe, that in republican Rome a citizen "was neither Caius nor Lucius; he was a Roman." (Bl.40, OC4.249) He forgot himself in identifying with his community. And without forgetting oneself, without sensing one's existence only in the social whole, one cannot transform dependence into freedom. In later chapters I shall argue that Rousseau recognizes in himself, what his account of the citizen denies, that the self cannot be forgotten. At Clarens, Wolmar, with Julie's aid, has created the facade of equality and unity. But the inhabitants of the estate retain their identities as masters and as servants. In the grape harvest the actors play their parts, but they do not forget either themselves or in the end, their selves.

From the estate let us turn to Julie's Elysium, described in the third of the ten letters that St. Preux writes from Clarens to Milord Edward. The Elysium is an orchard, or more accurately had been an orchard, metamorphosed so that St. Preux says that on entering it, "I thought I was looking at the wildest, most solitary place in nature, and it seemed to me I was the first mortal who ever had set foot in this wilderness." (CW6.387, OC2.471) He cried out, "Julie, the ends of the earth are at your gate!" But the ends of the earth, although hidden by "the heavy foliage surrounding [them]," are separated only by a shaded avenue from the house. "Many people find them [the ends of the earth] here as you do," Julie responded, "but twenty paces more bring them quickly back to Clarens." (Ibid.)

Only four keys open the gate to the Elysium; these are in the possession of Julie, Wolmar, Julie's father, and the children's governess, Fanchon. When St. Preux asks to be allowed to borrow Fanchon's key on occasion so that he might take on the task of feeding the birds that have been given a sanctuary in one of the far corners of the Elysium, Julie instead sends him her own. "I do

not know why I accepted it with some disappointment:" he tells
Edward, "it seemed to me I would rather have had Monsieur de
Wolmar's." (CW6.399, OC2.486)

The significance of the key will emerge more clearly as we
proceed. So let us continue with St. Preux's reactions as he first
saw the Elysium. It is a wilderness, but an artificial wilderness. He
did not realize this; "I see no human labor here," he said. "You
closed the gate," which we should note is always kept locked;
"water came along I know not how," for the previous orchard
was arid; "nature alone did the rest and you yourself could never
have managed to do as well." (CW6.388, OC2.472) But St. Preux
was mistaken. Julie agreed that "nature did it all, but under my
direction, and there is nothing here that I have not arranged."[20]
(Ibid.) The Elysium conveyed the appearance of being a wilderness, the effect of mere nature, but this was a contrived effect.
Contrasting the verdant site with the arid orchard that once occupied the spot, St. Preux admitted "there is something here I
cannot understand. It is that a place so different from what it
was could have become what it is only through cultivation and
upkeep; yet nowhere do I see the slightest trace of cultivation.
Everything is verdant, fresh, vigorous, and the gardener's hand is
not to be seen: nothing belies the idea of an uninhabited[21] Island
which came to my mind as I entered, and I see no human foot-
prints." Wolmar replied, "Ah! . . . that is because we have taken
great care to erase them. I have often been witness, sometimes
accomplice to the ruse."[22] (CW6.393, OC2.478–9) As the artifice
of the Tutor seeks to recreate a natural individual in the midst
of society, so Julie's artifice seeks to recreate a natural solitude in
the midst of habitation. Indeed, the Tutor could have used her
very words – "nature did it all, but under my direction, and there

---

[20] Tr., "designed"; Fr. "*ordonné.*"
[21] Tr., "desert"; Fr. "*déserte.*"
[22] Tr., "trickery"; Fr. "*fripponerie.*"

is nothing here that I have not arranged" – to describe his own work. And as the Tutor seeks to leave no trace of this work, so that Émile will not realize that his will has been made captive, so Julie seeks to leave no trace of her work. Recall Julie's account of their estate – "he [Wolmar] has so well ordained the original arrangement of things that now it runs all by itself" as he is the artificer of Clarens, so she is the artificer of the Elysium.

St. Preux was puzzled by this; he tells Edward, "I found it rather strange that they should take such pains to hide from themselves those they had taken." (CW6.394, OC2.479) Why take pains at all? But doing nothing would not have created the Elysium. Julie said, "[N]ature seems to want to veil from men's eyes her true attractions, . . . which they disfigure when they can get their hands on them." And so "she flees much-frequented places; it is on the tops of mountains, deep in the forests, on uninhabited[23] Islands that she deploys her most stirring charms." (Ibid.) Man disfigures nature as he disfigures himself. And for Rousseau it is clear that the men who are the least disfigured are those farthest from the crowd and the city – men who, like the peasants of the Swiss Vaud, inhabit the same mountains and forests that display nature's charms.

How then to find nature and live among her charms, if one "cannot go so far to find her"? "Those who love her," Julie acknowledged, are then "reduced to doing her violence, forcing her in a way to come and live with them, and all this cannot be done without a modicum of illusion." (CW6.394, OC2.479–80) Julie's words should give us pause. Illusion, as we noted in the first chapter, is one of the conditions that Rousseau contrasts with freedom. In Julie's Elysium, nature appears herself, but in conditions in which she cannot truly be herself. Julie is the demiurge of her Elysium. But since the Elysium is not the natural wilderness that it appears to be, Julie is not the demiurge

[23] Tr., "desert."

that she appears to be. She has created the illusion of a wilderness under the illusion that she has created a wilderness.

As his visit to Julie's Elysium was drawing to an end, St. Preux voiced a criticism – that it was superfluous, since there were charming bowers on the other side of the house. He was silenced by Wolmar, who pointed out to him that, since her marriage, Julie had not set foot in those bowers, and that, without her telling him, he, like St. Preux, knew the reason – which is, indeed, that in those other bowers the lovers first kissed. Wolmar told St. Preux to respect the ground of the Elysium; "it is planted by the hands of virtue." (CW6.398, OC2.485)

The next morning St. Preux, taking advantage of the key he had received, set out for the "uninhabited[24] Island." Now that he had learned that Julie was the source of its being, he thought, "My entire surroundings will be the handiwork of her whom I so cherished. . . . I shall see nothing that her hand has not touched. . . . I shall find her everywhere as she is deep in my heart." (CW6.399, OC2.486) But Wolmar's words came to his mind, and as he thought of virtue, his experience was transformed. He saw Julie as wife, as mother, as having established a sanctuary where one could be untroubled. He had gone to look for the handiwork of love; what he found were the fruits of virtue.

If they were the fruits of virtue. Doing violence to nature cannot be an innocent activity. Like the Tutor with Émile, Julie has sought to capture nature's "will," and to make it her own. She has countered nature's tendency to flee humankind, and directed its powers to her own ends. Her intent, no doubt, was to create a sanctuary, for herself and her family. But with the arrival of St. Preux, she has given up her key, her own right of entry, to that sanctuary. No longer is she free to enter the gate of paradise, without the company of her father, her husband, her children, or

[24] Tr., "desert."

her supposedly former lover. In depositing her key with St. Preux, she has symbolically given him equal status in her life with the other depositaries. But in depositing *her* key with him, she has removed the possibility that they might find themselves in Elysium together as the chance, or seemingly chance, outcome of separate intents. She has at once united herself with him by the gift of a key, and separated herself from him by the gift of *her* key.

Julie's Elysium is thus at the core of two, seemingly very different, accounts, both of which concern freedom. On the one hand, it exhibits the artifice of renaturalizing nature, of forcing nature, who "flees much-frequented places," to come and live *as nature* among men. It provides a comparison to the renaturalization of man, taking an individual, an Émile, and enabling him to live in the society of men, but as a *natural* man. Both nature and the individual need to be protected from disfigurement. But we must not overlook Julie's acknowledgement that we do violence to nature in bringing her to live among us; the Tutor does the same violence to Émile. And if Julie is able to create only the illusion of natural wilderness, then we might see this as confirmation that Rousseau's greater artificers can create only the illusion of human freedom.[25]

On the other hand, through the gift of the key the Elysium exhibits the painful ambiguity in the ongoing relationship between Julie and her former lover. St. Preux, of course, would have preferred Wolmar's key. He would have preferred to supplant Wolmar in his access to Julie's sanctuary, as he would have preferred to supplant him in access to Julie herself. He does

---

[25] Rousseau does not suggest that Julie's work is to *denature* nature; we should not then seek a direct parallel with the work of the Legislator. Perhaps we might compare his task, in taking from each person his own independent powers and replacing them with powers that can be used only collectively, with the work of those who create formal gardens, in which each individual plant or tree is ordered to the whole, and finds its place in the garden only insofar as it harmonizes with the other plants.

not know – or perhaps does not let himself know – this; hence his remark to Bomston that "I do not know why I accepted it [the key] with some disappointment." And Julie may equally not let herself know this. But of greater moment is the significance of the gift for herself – also something she may not let herself know. For if the Elysium symbolically signifies Julie herself, then in presenting her key to St. Preux she is giving possession of herself in a way that directly denies such possession, not only to St. Preux but also to herself. To regain her Elysium she now depends on others, the possessors of the keys, to whom she must in effect ask "Help me!" She no longer has a place of freedom. And she is no longer free in herself. In little more than a year the division in her soul between Mme. de Wolmar, mistress of Clarens, and Julie, lover of St. Preux, will reveal itself in her death.

At the core of *Julie* is Rousseau's understanding of love.[26] I shall claim that love is at the center of Rousseau's final attempt to redeem our fallen condition, and while this thesis may be controversial, it is hardly controversial that love is at the center of the novel. How are we to read its first words – "I must flee you, Mademoiselle" – but as a barely concealed form of that deep cry, *aimez-moi*. If the tutor meant to flee, he would have fled; he meant something else and so he wrote. And what he meant is surely not in doubt. What is in doubt is Julie's response to his cry – a response that, in effect, occupies the entire novel. But we need to know what love is, if we are to know what the tutor demands – and offers, and what Julie finally and irrevocably gives.

After Julie's marriage to Wolmar, and before her former lover puts to sea, she writes him, answering his question about her happiness, describing her husband and their life together, and

---

[26] This account of love is very different from that offered by the Tutor in *Emile*. I shall consider that other account again presently.

saying, "This is the last letter you shall receive from me. I beg you also to write me no more." (CW6.309, OC2.375) But when St. Preux has been admitted to Clarens, and then departs to assist Milord Edward in settling his affairs in Rome, Julie does write again, saying, "This is the first time in my life I have been able to write you without fear and without shame." (CW6.545, OC2.664) It is the letter in which she proposes that St. Preux consider marrying Claire. And St. Preux responds, ecstatically, "Julie! a letter from you! . . . after seven years of silence . . . yes it is she; I see it, I feel it: could my eyes mistake a hand my heart cannot forget?" (CW6.554, OC2.674) He has learned how to treat Julie as a friend, a mother, the wife of another, but his heart has only one response to her. And it is in this letter – a letter ostensibly about Julie's proposal, that he gives what I think is Rousseau's best and truest account of love. "But do two lovers love each other? No; *you* and *I* are words banished from their language; there are no longer two, they are one."[27] (CW6.555, OC2.675–6)

Our first sentiment is that of our existence. We begin, as individuals, and as a species, feeling that sentiment within ourselves. But as we mature, as we perfect ourselves, as we develop reason, we lose that internal sentiment. The natural human being is, after a brief childhood, self-sufficient; the social human being is not. He depends on others, physically and even more psychologically, so that he comes to sense his existence only in the opinions and attitudes of others. He is unfree; in himself he is nothing. *Emile*, I have argued, is Rousseau's failed attempt to create, within society, a man who is natural in being self-sufficient, and in sensing his existence within himself. The *Social Contract*, and the other political writings, are his attempt – also, as I have argued, and shall argue more fully in later chapters, failed – to create a society in which men are utterly dependent on the collective body of

---

[27] Thus love requires not merely mutual possession (contrary to the Tutor's advice to Émile discussed in Chapter 2) but mutual identification.

their fellows,[28] but in which they identify with this social whole of which they are part, and sense their existence in that whole. Love offers an alternative, in which two persons say not *aidez-moi* but *aimez-moi* to each other, and find a different form of dependence and identification, in which each senses his or her existence only in their union. "[T]here are no longer two, they are one." Freeing one from dependence on what is alien, love thus becomes the agent of redemption. Rousseau's citizen identifies with and is dependent on the whole that alone meets his demand for help. Rousseau's lover identifies with and is dependent on the pair of persons in which his or her demand for love is met. Describing Julie's dying days in his long, last letter to St. Preux, Wolmar quotes her: "I exist, I love, I am loved, I live till my last breath." (CW6.589, OC2.718) Julie's sentiment of existence is tied to loving and being loved.

Love involves the fusion of souls. Rousseau certainly suggests that friends who share their lives enjoy a degree of this fusion when, in the Second Preface to *Julie*, he observes "that in a very closely knit society, styles as well as characters become more like each other, and that friends, confounding their souls, also confound their manners of thinking, of feeling, and of speaking." (CW6.21, OC2.28) And some persons possess a magnetic effect on their associates. "Julie . . . must be an enchantress; everyone who comes near her is bound to resemble her; everyone about her is bound to become Julie." (Ibid.) If Wolmar is the designer of Clarens, Julie is its harmonic center. Julie's death will of course reveal a deeper disharmony. But the idea that friends enter into each other's sentiment of existence – an idea that we might relate to Aristotle's conception of the friend as "another self" – fits well with the account of lovers as not two but one.

In the letter to Julie where I have found the heart of this account, St. Preux also writes of his own condition. He tells Julie,

[28] But not dependent on their fellows individually, which would of course be slavery.

"[D]o not seek to save me from the nothingness into which I have fallen; lest with the sentiment of my existence I recover that of my woes." (CW6.559, OC2.681) St. Preux had united his existence with Julie's; deprived of that union, he has fallen into a nothingness that deprives him of his sentiment of existence. Here the deprivation is welcome, since to sense himself would be to sense his loss of himself. We should compare what St. Preux says here to his response to a much earlier letter from Julie – a letter, written after her recovery from smallpox and immediately before her marriage to Wolmar, in which she gives her lover her heart forever, while denying him her person. He replies, "We are coming back to life, my Julie; every true sentiment in our souls is resuming its course. Nature has preserved our being, and love is restoring us to life. . . . Thus we begin living again so as to begin suffering again, and the sentiment of our existence is for us but a sentiment of pain." (CW6.276, OC2.335–6) Here we have the lovers' sense of their existence as at once nourished by their love and fractured by their loss. Julie will, as we know, claim to be transformed by her wedding, finding duty to take the place of desire. We have yet to read Rousseau's last word on duty – that must await the *Reveries* – but we are, I think, now ready to consider Julie's.

She replies to St. Preux's impassioned letter; it is the day before her fatal accident. And her reply contains an extraordinary admission – sufficient to call for comment by Rousseau, in his role as editor of the letters. "My friend," she says, "I am too happy; I am weary of happiness" (CW6.570, OC2.694), and Rousseau comments editorially that "you are not, any longer, fully in accord with yourself." And prefiguring what is to come, he adds, "Besides, I admit that this letter seems to me the song of the swan."[29] This admission of Julie's is prefaced by a brief disquisition about happiness and desire. "Woe to him who has nothing

---

[29] These editorial comments are my translation.

left to desire!" Julie says. "One enjoys less what one obtains than what one hopes for, and one is happy only before happiness is achieved." (CW6.569, OC2.693) Desire gives the pleasure of imagination, embellishing the desired object, but "this whole spell disappears in the face of the object itself," so that "illusion ends where enjoyment begins." And then, in a claim that seems totally at odds with Rousseau's usual condemnation of illusion, she continues, "The land of chimeras[30] is on this earth the only one worth living in," and, making God an exception, "the only beauty to be found is in things that are not." (Ibid.)

Yet there is a further exception, for Julie immediately adds, "Although this effect does not always obtain for the particular objects of our passions, it never fails in the common sentiment that includes all passions." (CW6.570, OC2.693) What does Julie mean? What are the particular objects that escape the separation of imagination and enjoyment? The recent English translators of *Julie* are in no doubt. "The . . . preceding . . . thus concerns every passion but love, which on the contrary continues to fantasize the object of desire." (CW6.718) If this interpretation is right, it may seem to allow love the redemptive role I have claimed for it. But does it? Is not the claim here that love escapes the separation of imagination and enjoyment by preserving *illusion* even in the presence of the beloved? This may seem to make illusion part of the essence of love. And such an interpretation may seem to be confirmed by the passage from the Second Preface to the novel that I quoted in discussing the view of love presented in *Emile*, in which Rousseau himself says, "Love is but illusion; it fashions for itself, so to speak, another Universe; it surrounds itself with objects that do not exist, or to which it alone has given being. . . . It can see nothing but Paradise, . . . the delights of the celestial abode." (CW6.10, OC2.15–16). I shall need to return to this view of love as a form of illusion in discussing Rousseau's confessional

---

[30] Tr., "illusions"; Fr. "*chimeres.*"

writings. But at the end of the novel itself love emerges without illusion. Rousseau's statement in the Second Preface fails to capture love's transfiguration in Julie's death.

For although Julie claims the land of chimeras is the only one worth living in, this claim, I suggest, is itself part of the illusion from which she will free herself in her last words. In the land of chimeras she is too happy. The words "*trop heureuse*" will shortly recur, but with a very different meaning. From Julie wearied by her contentment we turn to Julie dying, and in her death finally aware of the true self that she believed had been transformed in her marriage, the self that was the source of her ennui. "For a long time I have lived an illusion." (OC2.740, my trans.)[31] Central to that illusion was surely her belief that she and Wolmar were "destined to constitute but a single soul." (CW6.307, OC2.374) But now the illusion is past. What Julie now recognizes is not that she has mistaken her duty, or been misled by a false conception of virtue. In death she does not renounce the actual life she has lived. But what she understands is that in that life she was not truly and fully herself – that its contentment was an illusion. To be herself she cannot renounce; she can only transcend. She cannot desert her husband and her children in life, but she can leave them in death. And that death offers what her life has denied her. "The virtue that separated us on earth shall unite us in the eternal abode." (CW6.610, OC2.743) In that eternal abode there can be no illusion, no mistaking the beloved for a chimerical ideal. And in that abode the two lovers will be one.

The novel begins with the tutor's cry for love, disguised as the insistence that he must flee Julie. It ends with the anticipation of the lovers' reunion, disguised as Julie's departure. "No, I am not leaving you, I go to await you. . . . I die in this sweet expectation." (OC2.743, my trans.)[32] And now the words "*trop heureuse*"

---

[31] Revised from Stewart and Vaché tr.; see note 3 above.
[32] Revised from Stewart and Vaché tr.; see notes 6, 8–11 above.

that Julie spoke in her ennui recur with a very different meaning, "Only too happy to purchase at the price of my life the right
to love you forever without crime." (Ibid.) Julie's life had been
sated with contentment; in dying, she transcends happiness for a
love that is not illusion but rather has been awakened from illusion. Julie and St. Preux will be united in "the eternal abode."
Starobinski understands Rousseau's thought in terms of an alter-
nation of transparency and obstruction; here we would seem to
have – and I think do have – one of the few moments of full
transparency.

I have spoken of love as redemptive because it promises to
bring lovers into a union in which each senses his or her existence
in common with the other, and is fulfilled by that identification.
"Redemption" may seem too strong a word for Julie and St. Preux,
who are not debilitated by *amour propre*. Nevertheless, each needs
the completion of the other; Julie speaks of her ennui, St. Preux
of his nothingness, in their everyday lives. But whether love is an
answer to the fallen condition Rousseau describes in the *Second
Discourse* is hardly answered by the novel; that is a subject for later
chapters. I want to conclude this discussion by reflecting on the
significance of Julie's death for Rousseau's system of thought.
First of all, it seems clear that her death shows the failure of
Wolmar's efforts to create an ideal community. It is, after all, that
community that Julie eventually finds wearisome. The happiness
of Clarens, like its equality, is a facade. Wolmar seeks to cure Julie
and St. Preux of their dependence on each other so that they can
live as friends; it seems clear that love, and not friendship, is what
they require – indeed, is what expresses their being. Second, it
seems clear that Julie's death shows the impossibility of uniting
love to duty and virtue without transcending the limits of this
world. Julie's illusion led her to believe that she could be fulfilled
by duty, virtue, and friendship. When these prove insufficient,
she can avoid renouncing them only by renouncing instead her
life. In this way virtue can comport with duty here, and with love

hereafter. But we may ask whether this resolution suffices for St. Preux, whose situation is left emotionally unresolved.

Wolmar, who sends St. Preux Julie's last letter enclosed in his long account of her death, has been an atheist – the one aspect of his character that had always troubled Julie. As he recounts Julie giving him her letter, wanting him to read it once she is dead and then to decide whether to send it, he says, "However much I know that she who wrote it is dead, I have difficulty believing there is nothing left of her." (CW6.591, OC2.720) Wolmar sought to order their earthly lives; reading Julie's letter could not but make him aware of his failure. His belief in the possibility of order may be stronger than his disbelief in another world. But if another world is needed for our souls to find the order they seek, then Rousseau's artificers have no remedy for the ills of the human condition.

5

Making Jean-Jacques

"Let the trumpet of the last judgement sound when it will; I shall come with this book in my hands to present myself before the Sovereign Judge." (CW5.5, OC1.5) "This book" is of course the *Confessions*. "I shall say loudly, 'Behold what I have done, what I have thought, what I have been.'" And if there is a gap in memory, "I may have assumed to be true what I knew might have been so, never what I knew to be false." So in the *Confessions*, Rousseau presents himself for judgment. And not only by the sovereign judge, for he demands, "Eternal Being, assemble around me the countless host of my fellows: let them listen to my confessions, let them shudder at my unworthiness, let them blush at my woes . . . and then let a single one say to Thee, if he dares: '*I was better than that man.*'" (Ibid.)

But the *Confessions* does more than present Rousseau for judgment. In the note found in the Geneva manuscript of the *Confessions*, he announces, "Here is the only portrait of a man, painted exactly according to nature and in all its truth, that exists and that will probably ever exist." (CW5.3, OC1.3) He pleads with whoever decides its fate, "not to destroy a unique and useful work, a study which can serve as the first comparative base[1] for the study of men, which certainly has not yet begun." The *Confessions* is then

---

[1] Kelly tr., "piece of comparison"; Fr. "*piéce de comparaison.*"

a document, the first and perhaps only one of its kind, for an anthropology *yet to be undertaken.* And yet Rousseau is the author of the *Discourse on Inequality*, which he describes to his fellows as "your history as I believed I read it[2] . . . in Nature." (CW3.19, OC3.133) Did it not begin the study of humankind? Or does Rousseau implicitly distinguish two studies – one beginning with the species, the other with the individual?

The *Confessions* is "the only portrait of a man, painted exactly according to nature." But it is also the portrait of Rousseau alone, for he says, "I am not made like any of the ones I have seen; I dare to believe that I am not made like any that exist. If I am worth no more, at least I am different." (CW5.5, OC1.5) So the *Confessions* is unique both for its truth as a portrait, and for the nature of the man it portrays. And although the man is unique, the portrait can yet "serve as the first comparative base for the study of men."

The *Confessions* is a portrait that is to be faithful to its subject – it is to be true to Rousseau. But it is also a portrait to be executed in a way faithful to nature. If only what is true to nature can be represented according to nature, then for the two fidelities to hold, Rousseau must himself be true to nature. And since Rousseau is different, by implication other men are *not* true to nature – a view that Rousseau certainly held. But then the *Confessions* is the portrait of the only man true to nature, and so the only portrait true to nature. The unique truth of the *Confessions* depends on the unique truth of the confessor. And its usefulness as "the first comparative base" depends also on the unique truth of the confessor. If it is the only, then it is of course also the first work in which a man true to nature is depicted, and so it provides the model with which all other representations of human beings may be compared. Like Rousseau's educational and social writings, the *Confessions* is a normative study.

[2] Bush tr., "believed it to read."

Confession *and* anthropological study. Basis for evaluating the worth of the man *and* the only portrait of a man drawn in accordance with nature. Does Rousseau sustain these juxtapositions? Pursuing this question, I shall be led to other questions. In portraying himself, does Rousseau write an illusion? And can the portrait be finished? Or must the portrait remain incomplete – as his last writing, his last promenade, is incomplete? These are the underlying themes of the remaining chapters of my inquiry.

To mention the last promenade is to bring the *Reveries* into our picture. I read them as the further progression of the *Confessions*. In the first promenade Rousseau speaks of returning to "the severe and sincere examination I formerly called my *Confessions*. I consecrate my last days to studying myself and to preparing in advance the account I will give of myself before long." (CW8.6, OC1.999) But a little later, he tells us, "These pages can be considered, then, as an appendix to my *Confessions*; but I no longer give them that title, no longer feeling anything to say which merits it." (CW8.7, OC1.1000) The severe examination finds no more to censure, and so the past becomes the place of reverie, not confession.

Treating the *Confessions* and the *Reveries* together, I want to distance them from the third work that falls chronologically between them and is frequently taken as the third of Rousseau's primary autobiographical texts. The *Dialogues: Rousseau Judge of Jean-Jacques* is written to a different end. Whereas the *Confessions* is written *for* judgment, and the *Reveries* is, as it were, beyond judgment, the *Dialogues* is a work *of* judgment. It is not a work in which Rousseau examines or expresses himself, but in which Jean-Jacques is examined and judged, a work written in the third, not the first person. Although Rousseau is one of the judges, his persona in the *Dialogues* is kept distinct from that of Jean-Jacques, the judged, so that the work is not internally reflexive. The *Confessions* and the *Reveries* present themselves as works of self-examination, the latter in some sense following on from the former; the *Dialogues* presents itself as a third-party inquiry. To place it between the other two works, and then to take the ensemble as a whole in which a single theme is to be discerned, is to invite misunderstanding of what I shall call Rousseau's confessional project. I have already made references to the *Dialogues*, and I shall of course continue to do so. But in my reading of Rousseau, I find it standing outside Rousseau's construction of himself in the autobiographical writings. Indeed, I read it as primarily a deconstructive work, revealing, despite its underlying paranoia, Rousseau's deep understanding of the implications of his accounts of individual and collective redemption. Here then I put it to one side.

So let us begin our examination of the portrait with Rousseau as a child. "I felt before thinking; this is the common fate of humanity. I experienced it more than others. I am not aware of what I did up to the age of five or six: I do not know how I learned to read; I remember only my first readings and their effect on me. This is the time from which I date the uninterrupted consciousness of myself." (CW5.7, OC1.8) The sentiment of existence, as Rousseau insists in the *Discourse on Inequality*, is natural to man and is felt rather than thought; it has no temporality. Rousseau's emphasis on the priority of feeling, as the common lot of men but as more pronounced in his own case than in others, should I think be read as a sign of his own identification with natural or original man – an identification that he denies to his fellows. Unbroken temporal consciousness of the self, a far more complex phenomenon than the mere sentiment of existence, is introduced as a response to *written* language. Words provide the fabric of human existence; we have seen the relation between man's first words, *aimez-moi* and *aidez-moi*, and the development of *amour propre*. Here we see that the sense of the fixity or permanence of our existence requires the fixity of words in writing. Rousseau came to consciousness of himself through reading; I understand him to be defining that consciousness in his confessional writing.

Aimez-moi offers itself as the theme of the first part of the *Confessions*. Speaking of himself as a child, Rousseau says, "To be loved by everyone who approached me was my keenest desire." (CW5.12, OC1.14) His world is already filled with women – Mlle. Lambercier, Mlle. Goton, Mlle. de Vulson – objects of a precocious and oblique sexual appetite. Mlle. Lambercier, sister of the pastor with whom the young Jean-Jacques and his cousin boarded for two years (Rousseau's mother died in giving birth to him), inadvertently introduced him to sensuality by punishing him. He tells us that his greatest desires were "[t]o be on my knees before an imperious mistress, to obey her orders, to ask her for forgiveness." (CW5.15, OC1.17) Slavery enters early into Rousseau's life, and affects all that follows. But we should not deny the presence of true love, and indeed we must find out how it arises, for only by understanding Rousseau's entry into love shall we understand Rousseau's final sentiment of his own existence and the account that he leaves us, perhaps in spite of himself, of human nature.

Jean-Jacques met his first loves, Mlle. de Vulson and Mlle. Goton, at Nyon, while visiting his father, who had been obliged to leave Geneva as the result of a quarrel. As he was but twelve and Mlle. de Vulson twenty-two,[3] we may find his account of mutual affection somewhat suspect, as indeed he himself does, but what is of primary interest to our inquiry is not the details of his descriptions but rather the way in which he characterizes the two relationships. For he says, "I know two sorts of love which are very distinct, very real, and which have almost nothing in common, although both are very lively and both differ from tender friendship. The whole course of my life has been divided between these two loves of such different natures, and I have even experienced both of them at the same time." (CW5.23, OC1.27). In the earlier Neuchâtel manuscript of the *Confessions* Rousseau is

---

[3] We do not know Mlle. Goton's age, although she was clearly much younger than Mlle. de Vulson.

more specific: "the one sensuous, or from temperament, and the other Platonic, or from opinion." (CW5 notes.603) His love of Mlle. Goton was sensuous, of Mlle. de Vulson platonic, passionate,[4] but cerebral. We shall return to this distinction between sensuous and cerebral love. But now let us follow Jean-Jacques' adventures, as he comes to leave his native city and try to make his way in the world.

We must then see him at sixteen, somewhat unwillingly apprenticed to an engraver, whose authority he found – as throughout his life he found all actual authority – unreasonably constraining. On Sundays after the obligatory Calvinist services Jean-Jacques, in the company of other youths, went out into the countryside. At nightfall the gates of Geneva were locked; twice Rousseau had found himself outside, and faced severe punishment from his master. He knew that the third time would be much worse; nevertheless, once again he found himself outside. And so he decided to quit Geneva, and make his way in the world: "by merely showing myself I was going to occupy the universe with me." (CW5.38, OC1.45) Rousseau arrived at Confignon, a town in Savoy (then part of the domains of the king of Sardinia) some six miles from Geneva, and met the local priest, who shrewdly recognized an opportunity to make a convert from Calvinism to Catholicism. "God calls you," he said. "Go to Annecy; there you will find a very charitable good Lady, whom the good deeds of the King put in a position to save other souls from the error from which she herself has departed." (CW5.40, OC1.47) And the priest gave the young lad his letter of recommendation.

So Rousseau went to Annecy. "Finally I arrive; I see Mme de Warens."[5] (CW5.40, OC1.48) In these words he begins his

---

[4] "[W]e wrote each other letters of a pathos that could make rocks split." (CW5.25, OC1.29)

[5] Françoise-Louise de La Tour, Baronne de Warens, referred to by Rousseau as Louise Éleonor de Warens, estranged from her Protestant Swiss husband,

account of the meeting to which he will return in the final promenade. But he has – and we have – far to go before that return.
"Finally I arrive; I see Mme. de Warens. This epoch of my life
determined my character; I cannot resolve to pass over it lightly."
How does Rousseau tell us about this encounter? First by describing his own appearance, the appearance that we may suppose
would have determined Madame de Warens' immediate impression of him, and then telling us, "Unfortunately I knew nothing
about all that." And so, fearful that his looks would not gain her
favor, he had written her a letter – "a fine letter in the style of
an Orator" (CW5.41, OC1.48) in which phrases borrowed from
books were joined to the language of an apprentice. He reached
her house, letter in hand, to find her departed for church. He ran
after her. About to enter the church door, she turned to face him
at his call. "I ought to remember the place; since that time I have
often watered it with my tears and covered it with my kisses. . . .
Whoever loves to honor the monuments of men's salvation ought
to approach it only on his knees." (CW5.41, OC1.48–9) His first
look saw all. "Nothing escaped the rapid glance of the young
proselyte, for I became hers at that moment."

In that instant Rousseau was born to the woman he always
called "Maman," even when, years later, they became lovers.
And *maman* becomes the principal character (other than Jean-
Jacques) in the first part of the *Confessions*. But only in the first
part. In its penultimate paragraph we find Rousseau "building

convert to Catholicism, and pensioner of the king of Sardinia (and other
notables), is in her own right a quite interesting and even remarkable figure,
although our concern with her is limited to her relationship with Rousseau,
as he portrays it in the *Confessions* and the *Reveries*. Resident in Savoy (which
the king of Sardinia ruled as duke), she was an active proselytizer for the
Catholic faction, a consistently unsuccessful but always hopeful entrepreneur,
and apparently, an occasional participant in somewhat shadowy political and
diplomatic schemes. She enjoyed the company of young men, whom she happily bedded without scruple. She was thirteen years older than Rousseau – at
the time of their first meeting, twenty-nine to his sixteen.

new Castles in Spain to extricate that poor Mamma from the cruel extremities into which I saw her ready to fall." (CW5.221, OC1.279) His dreaming is interrupted by the thought of a more definite project, to make his fortune (and with it hers) by reforming the system of musical notation. And with this (unsuccessful) reform in mind, he departed for Paris and out of Madame de Warens's life.

But I am getting ahead of my story. Let us return to the young Jean-Jacques, spellbound, handing Madame de Warens his letter, together with the priest's recommendation. These read, Madame de Warens sent him home to await her return from church. Rousseau takes advantage of this interlude to describe her appearance, her education, her character, her activities, and to reflect on his relationship with her. The reflection will be important to us presently. The immediate question was what was to become of Jean-Jacques, and this was settled over dinner. He told her his story; to do this he "found again all the fire"[6] lost at his master's. (CW5.44, OC1.53) When this was done, the "Boor" (as Rousseau calls him) with whom they were dining proposed that Jean-Jacques should proceed to Turin to be prepared for conversion. Madame de Warens, in effect a paid recruiter for the Catholic faith, could hardly object to the proposal,[7] and Jean-Jacques was far too smitten to offer any opposition. And so he went to Turin, abjuring his Protestant faith, and with it his right to Genevan citizenship, only a month after his arrival in Annecy.

We should not think that, when Rousseau identifies the place where he first saw Madame de Warens as one of "the monuments

---

[6] The Paris manuscript of the *Confessions* reads, "found again all the fire which Mlle. de Vulson had inspired in me." (See note in OC1.1258.) This would be the first indication that Jean-Jacques' affection for Mme. de Warens was also of the Platonic or cerebral type.

[7] And indeed, in reality she may have made the proposal. Rousseau may well have wanted to ascribe the idea to another, to suggest that Madame de Warens would, even on such short acquaintance, have preferred to keep him with her.

of men's salvation," he had this conversion in mind – indeed, of course, he later resumed his original Protestantism. The salvation of which he speaks is rather the redemptive transformation *maman* made in his life. But we might question whether we should take this reference at face value. For Rousseau is disposed to ascribe degrees of significance to many of the events he relates in the *Confessions* that we may find inflationary or hyperbolic. Relating his punishment by Mlle. Lambercier, he writes, "Who would believe that this childhood punishment received at eight years of age from the hand of a woman of thirty determined my tastes, my desires, my passions, my self for the rest of my life . . .?" (CW5.13, OC1.15) Not everything can have determined his very self, and so we need to proceed with caution in attempting to fix the significance of his first encounter with Madame de Warens, and not simply trust his reference to salvation and his claim that "[t]his epoch of my life determined my character." (CW5.40, OC1.48) But the relationship between Jean-Jacques and Madame de Warens that is portrayed in the *Confessions*, and his final memories in the last promenade beginning with the Palm Sunday on which he met her, will give his claim the support it needs, and will justify our closer inquiry into Rousseau's narration of the events of that first day. Taking this as a promissory note, I want to reflect on how he begins.

Jean-Jacques arrives; he sees Madame de Warens. But as I have already noted, he does not proceed immediately to tell us what or whom he sees. Instead, he provides the first description in the *Confessions* of his own appearance, of how he is seen. It is only when Jean-Jacques meets Madame de Warens, and so sees and *is seen by* her, that Rousseau represents himself as existing *for another* by describing his appearance. Previously the young Jean-Jacques has existed only for himself. As he walked gaily from Geneva to Confignon, he viewed the world as an extension of himself, filling it with his fame, finding "feasts, treasures, adventures, friends ready to serve me, mistresses eager to please me."

(CW5.38, OC1.45) Now he viewed himself as the world, and most especially as Madame de Warens, would see him. In coming to exist for another, the primary unself-conscious concern motivating actions based on our natural needs, *amour de soi*, begins to transform itself into *amour propre*, the secondary self-conscious concern motivating actions based on our appearance to others. Rousseau's description of the youth Jean-Jacques records the beginning of this transformation in himself, in the moment in which he encounters Madame de Warens.[8] The message conveyed first in this description is then reiterated explicitly in the subsequent narrative; recalling the meeting he exclaims, "What becomes of me at that sight!" and again, "I became hers at that moment." (CW5.41, OC1.49) Jean-Jacques has passed from the self-sufficient youth ready to hazard all in turning his back on Geneva, to the dependent proselyte of the charitable lady. Has he lost his natural liberty? Or has he found liberty in a new form?

But after describing his young self, Rousseau insists that he was quite unaware of his appearance. In approaching Madame de Warens, he did not know what it was to exist for another. And so rather than offer his appearance, he prepared the fine letter – the first of his authorial acts.[9] But what he wrote could only have been the self he was, and not the self he became in the moment of meeting Madame de Warens. Fortunately, she could see the person and not just the letter. She could see the person who had become hers. What we need to ask, although we cannot yet offer an answer, is whether the person she could see was the real

---

[8] Perhaps we should see the transformation foreshadowed in his relationship with Mlle. de Vulson, when he says, "[W]ith pride I triumphed from her preference in front of great rivals." (CW5.24, OC1.28) In note 6 above I suggested that Rousseau's relationship with Mme. de Warens was similar in kind to that with Mlle. de Vulson.

[9] In the account of his childhood, Rousseau mentions writing in but one context: "when my theme was written, I helped him [my cousin Bernard] to do his." (CW5.12, OC1.13)

Jean-Jacques. In coming to exist for her, had he ceased to exist for himself?

Jean-Jacques arrives; he sees Madame de Warens. She was not yet *maman*, nor he, as he came to be, *petit*, little one – the first meeting was too brief to establish this relationship. But the very word that he came to adopt for her when he returned to live in her household emphasizes the dependence that, I am claiming, began in that first moment in which he came to exist for her. However, it is not the dependence that, beginning with the words *aidez-moi*, culminates in one's very sentiment of existence becoming hostage to the alien wills of one's fellows. Nor is it the dependence of Émile on the Tutor, or of the Citizen on the Legislator, although her role in forming the young Jean-Jacques is in important ways analogous to the Tutor's role in forming Émile, and to the Legislator's in forming the Citizen. To understand Rousseau's peculiar dependence on *maman*, I shall trace the course of their relationship, and then quote at length and with interspersed comments the passage from the *Confessions* in which his dependence is most fully revealed.

Jean-Jacques' first stay with Madame de Warens was very brief, from Palm Sunday until the following Wednesday, when he departed for Turin. After his conversion, he remained for over a year, most of the time in service, until he threw over his position and returned to Annecy. "Behold me then finally established in her home." (CW5.87, OC1.104) And during the next year Madame de Warens effectively took charge of his life, although for most of the time he did not actually live in her household. But this period of his life ended unexpectedly when, returning to Annecy from a mission to Lyon on which Madame de Warens had sent him, he found her gone. More than a year passed – a year spent largely in Lausanne, Neuchâtel, and Paris, and one that will require some attention in the next chapter when we examine a quite different aspect of Rousseau's life, his disguises. But learning that Madame de Warens was in Chambéry, Jean-Jacques returned to her, where he would spend the next six years, "the happy days of my life" (ibid.) as her companion and, in time, her lover.[10]

Let us now turn to Rousseau's fullest account of their relationship during the happy years in Chambéry, and at Madame de Warens' country retreat, Les Charmettes.

Our mutual attachment did not increase . . . , that was not possible; but it acquired an indefinable something that was more intimate, more touching in its great simplicity. I became completely her work, completely her child and more than if she had been my true mother. [Need I emphasize the passivity explicitly acknowledged in the child-mother relationship?] Without thinking about it we began no longer to distinguish ourselves one from the other,[11] so as to put our whole existence in common in some way [existing in common should be contrasted to the various other ways in which Rousseau claims that we may experience our existence], and feeling that we were reciprocally not only necessary but sufficient for each other, we accustomed ourselves to thinking about nothing that was foreign to us any longer, to limiting our happiness and all our desires absolutely to that possession that was mutual and perhaps unique among humans [here Rousseau specifies the psychologically sufficient entity – in this case the pair, Jean-Jacques and *maman*, which we should contrast with the unit, natural man, and the whole, the society of citizens]; which was not . . . that of love; but a more essential possession which – without depending on the senses, on sex, on age, on looks – depended on everything by which one is oneself, and which one cannot lose without ceasing to be. (CW5.186, OC1.222)

This last sentence poses two deeply problematic issues. One is to understand the connection between this "essential possession" and the sentiment of existence. On one parsing of the last part of this sentence, taking the final "which" to refer back

---

[10] And indeed, Rousseau would spend much of four more years in Chambéry, although no longer as Madame de Warens' intimate. We shall see later how the period of intimacy ended; the years in Chambéry that follow receive the briefest of treatments in the *Confessions*.

[11] Kelly tr., "not to separate from each other any more."

to "possession," Rousseau would be claiming that the relationship between Jean-Jacques and *maman* was essential to their very being. On the alternative parsing, taking the final "which" to refer back to "everything," Rousseau would be claiming that the relationship depended on what was essential to their existence, and so, I think we may infer, what was itself an essential part of their sentiment of existence, their sense of themselves. Since the relationship did not endure, we shall have to examine how its ending affected Jean-Jacques' sense of his existence.[12]

The other issue is the relation between love and "essential possession," which are here contrasted. We need to examine once again Rousseau's conception of love, and ask how it relates to the mutual possession of Jean-Jacques and *maman*. We are seeking the deep meaning of the first words of the southern languages – the magical phrase *aimez-moi* that expresses the young Jean-Jacques' liveliest desire. That this is his desire, so that humankind's first words are also his, is at the core of his self-conception. To begin our search we need to return to Rousseau's account of Jean-Jacques' first encounter with *maman*, and to his reflections on their relationship that I mentioned previously but deferred. For here we find love put in question.

Let us assume that what I felt for her was genuinely love; which will appear at least doubtful to anyone who follows the history of our relations; how did it happen that from its birth this passion was accompanied by the feelings it inspires least; peace of heart, calm, serenity, security, certainty? . . . Does one have love, I do not say without desires – I had them – but without restlessness, without jealousy? (CW5.43–4, OC1.52)

---

[12] Should we also ask how *maman* might have regarded these words of her little one? Recall that my concern is with the persons Rousseau creates. That the historical person, the Baronne de Warens, might have written a very different account of her relationship to the person she called "*Petit*" and who called her "*Maman*" is of no direct relevance.

The association of love with disquiet and jealousy would suggest that for Rousseau, it would be natural to correlate love with a desire for the exclusive possession of the beloved and her affections – for control over her desires and will. And this would make it a relationship of enslavement. But we may instead understand Jean-Jacques' desire as being, certainly for possession of *maman*, but as identification with her rather than as control over her. In the fusion of persons that Rousseau envisages, there is but one set of desires and one will. And this fusion has no place for disquiet or jealousy – the presence of either would reveal that the appearance of fusion was illusory. We may then suppose that Rousseau's ambiguous reference to love should lead us to recognize the imperfection in the ordinary form of that emotion – the dependence of the lover on the desires and will of his beloved, which are beyond his control. Such a lover is unfree, in his psychological dependence on that which remains alien to him. Jean-Jacques, on the other hand, depends only on that with which he is one, and so is free in his relationship with *maman*.

Love is an expression of *amour propre*; it depends on the recognition of the other. But love as identification cancels the self-other distinction, integrating lover and beloved, self and other, into one. Recall St. Preux's words to Julie, "*[Y]ou* and *I* are words banished from their [the lovers'] language." (CW6.555, OC2.676) And so love becomes an expansion of *amour de soi* into *amour de nous*, or perhaps better, *amour chez nous*. The lovers exist in mutual recognition.

Rousseau asks, "Does one not wish at least to learn from the object one loves whether one is loved? This is a question which it no more entered my mind to ask her once in my life, than to ask myself whether I loved myself, and she was never any more curious with me." (CW5.44, OC1.52) If Jean-Jacques truly sought, and believed that he had found, the fusion of his person with that of his *maman*, then questions of being loved and loving should no more have arisen than the question of being loved by and loving one's self. To ask about one's own self-love is to recognize the fissure of self-estrangement. No similar fault line should mar the seamless whole that Rousseau creates.

Later, after referring to "the sweet habit of the affectionate feelings with which she inspired me," he tells us, "I will dare to say it; whoever feels only love does not feel what is sweetest in life. I am acquainted with another feeling" (CW5.87, OC1.104), and after attempting to describe it, he concludes, "This is not clear, but it will become so in what follows; feelings are described well only through their effects." (CW5.88, OC1.104) The effects to which he refers are surely found in the description he gives of Jean-Jacques' life with *maman*, and especially the passage that I have quoted, which gave rise to this discussion of love. What goes beyond love is "a more essential possession" in which the two "put [their] whole existence in common," so that, as St. Preux insists, "there are no longer two, they are one." (CW6.555, OC2.676)

This "more essential possession" is Rousseau's greatest need. In Book 9, in the second part of the *Confessions*, he writes,

> The first of my needs, the greatest, the strongest, the most inextinguish-able, was entirely in my heart: it was the need for an intimate society and as intimate as it could be; it was above all for this that I needed a woman rather than a man, 'une amie' more than 'un ami'.[13] This peculiar need was such that the closest union of bodies could not even be enough for it: I would have needed two souls in the same body; since I did not have that, I always felt some void. (CW5.348, OC1.414)

He wrote this of a time when his union with Madame de Warens was long past, and when his attempts to fill the void in his life led him to take Thérèse Levasseur as his companion. We shall consider his relationship with her presently.

Two more references to love in the first part of the *Confessions* demand our attention next. These both occur between

---

[13] Kelly tr., "a lover rather than a friend."

Rousseau's first mention of "another feeling" and his later clari-
fication. In the first, he notes that

My attachment for her [*maman*] . . . did not keep me from loving others,
but not in the same way. All equally owed my tenderness to their charms,
but with others it depended solely on their charms, . . . whereas mamma
could become old and ugly without me loving her any less tenderly. My
heart had fully transferred to her person the homage that it gave to her
beauty at first. (CW5.126, OC1.151)

And Rousseau goes on to note that although he "owed her
gratitude," yet "[w]hatever she might have done or not done for
me, it would always have been the same thing. I loved her neither
out of duty, nor out of interest, nor out of convenience; I loved
her because I was born to love her." The man who feels no more
than love is smitten by the charms he ascribes to his beloved, and
is enslaved by the desire to possess them, but the man who loves
the *person* of his beloved seeks identification with her, and this
expresses his true self – he is by nature "born to love her" as man
is by nature "born free." (CW4.131, OC3.353) The third way[14] to
seek to escape from slavish dependence is the way of the lover –
if we understand the lover as expressing the desire to exist as one
with the person of the beloved.

The second reference to love relates it to sexual desire.
Rousseau's relationship with Madame de Warens was more than
a communion of souls; he came to share her bed – although until
the death of her steward, Claude Anet, he was not her only part-
ner. But physical possession was never at the core of their relationship, at least insofar as Rousseau represented it. Although
when he first met Madame de Warens at Annecy he "was intoxicated," later, "at Chambéry I no longer was. I always loved her
as passionately as possible, but I loved her more for herself and

---

[14] The first two that Rousseau identifies are, of course, the creation of an Émile,
a natural man in society, and the creation of citizens. If these fail, does the
creation of a lover succeed?

less for me, or at least I looked more for my happiness than my pleasure with her. . . . In sum, I loved her too much to covet her: that is what is clearest in my ideas." (CW5.165, OC1.196–7) When Rousseau did possess her physically, he tells us, "I imagined [a mistress] in her place." (CW5.183, OC1.219) The moment of sexual possession was not one of existential identification.

Indeed, there are passages in the *Confessions* which may suggest that the very physical presence of Madame de Warens impeded Rousseau's identification with her. Writing of the period when he first lived in her household, though not yet sharing her bed, Rousseau tells us, "I felt all the strength of my attachment for her only when I did not see her. When I saw her I was only content; but my uneasiness in her absence went so far as to be painful." (CW5.90, OC1.107) Later, when he is about to share her bed, he writes "I was well off only near her; . . . I went away from her only to think about her." (CW5.163, OC1.195) But in this later passage there is no suggestion that he was *merely* happy when beside her. And later still, at the time at which Rousseau represents them as sharing their "existence in common," their presence to each other is clearly essential. We should not expect Rousseau to treat a true existential union between Jean-Jacques and *maman* as if it were an exercise of imagination, even if the mutual identification that constitutes it does not require, and is even impeded by, sexual possession.[15]

As I have noted, Rousseau distinguishes two forms of love at the outset of the *Confessions*, sensuous and platonic. Much that he says in differentiating his attachment to Mme. de Warens from love, would seem to distinguish it from sensuous love. And certainly his attachment to her was not primarily sensuous. But even

---

[15] Of course, whether Rousseau's account of the existential union between Jean-Jacques and Madame de Warens is no more than an exercise of authorial imagination is a quite separate issue, and not one that I am attempting to examine here.

platonic love, as Rousseau understands it, is less than his attachment to *maman*, since it does not entail the union of the lovers. I have argued that there is a further distinction between forms of love in the *Confessions* – between love as the desire to possess exclusively the affections of the beloved and love as the desire to identify one's existence with that of the beloved. I have found this latter form of love in two key relationships, between St. Preux and Julie and between Jean-Jacques and Madame de Warens. In the second chapter we saw that Émile's Tutor discusses love in quite different terms, calling "true love itself . . . chimera, lie, and illusion." (Bl.329, OC4.656) And this account of love we found repeated in the Second Preface to *Julie*. What is not illusory, on this view, are our sentiments for "the truly beautiful" (Bl.391, OC4.743) that is the ideal object of our love; what is illusory is the supposition that this beauty is in the actual beloved. But this illusion would seem to depend on recognizing the beloved as other, since the lover does not identify *himself* with the beauty he adores. If there is an illusion present in existential identification, it is different, and indeed deeper. Jean-Jacques saw his *maman*, not as beauty incarnate, but as essential to his true self, and existing in common with him.

Rousseau does relate beauty and existential identification in one of his most remarkable writings, the brief lyrical scene *Pygmalion*, performed at the Paris Opera in 1772. Pygmalion looks at his statue of Galatea, and exclaims, "I am transported by *amour propre*; I adore myself in what I have done." (OC2.1226)[16] But then he realizes, "It isn't this dead marble for which I am smitten; it's for a living being who resembles it." (OC2.1227) He wants to give the statue his life and his soul – "let Pygmalion die so that he may live in Galatea." (OC2.1228) But then he draws back; "If I were she, I shouldn't see her, I shouldn't be he who loves her. . . . Let me be always another, in order always to wish to be her, to see

---

[16] Translations from *Pygmalion* are mine. There is a translation by Kelly in CW10.

her, to love her, to be loved by her. . . ." And finally he calls out to the goddess of beauty, "Spare nature this affront, that such a perfect model be the image of what does not exist." (OC2.1229) Galatea then comes to life. She touches herself and says, "Me." (OC2.1230) Transported, Pygmalion repeats, "Me!" She walks over and touches a marble; "It isn't me." Then she comes toward Pygmalion and touches him; "Ah! me again." (OC2.1231) And Pygmalion responds, "It's you, it's you alone: I've given you all my being; I no longer live but through [*par*] you." (Ibid.) Beyond *amour propre*, Pygmalion has become what he has created. He has identified with beauty.

Pygmalion is clearly a special and indeed unique case. His love is narcissistic; he adores himself in what he has done. He identifies with beauty because it is his own creation. His love embraces elements of all of the conceptions of love that we have found in Rousseau's writings, but in altered form. He worships the beauty he has created, but this is not an ideal beauty falsely projected onto an unworthy object; he is not in this way the victim of illusion. He identifies his own existence with that of Galatea, but this is not, as with St. Preux and Julie or Jean-Jacques and Madame de Warens, the union of two persons into a single whole, but the absorption of one person into his own creation. And he seeks possession, not so that he may possess his beloved, but so that he may be possessed by her – indeed annulled. He wants to be other than Galatea only so that he can wish to be her, but such an existence would be self-annihilating. All that remains to him is to be Galatea, to live through (*par*) her.

But unique as Pygmalion is, the implications of his love are unsettling. His identification with Galatea takes the form of an abnegation of self. Does Jean-Jacques' identification with Madame de Warens involve a parallel abnegation? When we come to the last promenade – the object of our quest – we shall find that the text forces us to rethink the significance of Pygmalion's response to Galatea's touch, his acknowledgement that he no longer lives but through (*par*) her. In his relationship with Madame de Warens, Jean-Jacques seeks a condition of perfect freedom. I do not read Pygmalion's final words, responding to Galatea's touch, as a cry of freedom.

So has Rousseau written an illusion? We shall address this question in the final chapter. Here we need to consider the dénouement of our story, returning to the relationship that Rousseau represents between his younger self and Madame de Warens. And we find imagination and reality, dream and waking, interrelated. Immediately after recounting his painful disquiet in her absence – at a time, recall, when neither their existential nor their sexual union had been consummated – Rousseau proceeds to relate a solitary walk he took,

> my heart full of her image and of the ardent desire to pass my days near her. I had enough sense to see that at present this was not possible. . . . That gave my reverie a sadness that however had nothing somber about it and that was tempered by a flattering hope. . . . I saw myself carried away as if in ecstasy to that happy time and into that happy abode. . . . I do not remember ever launching myself into the future with more force and illusion than I did then; and what struck me most in the remembrance of this reverie when it came true, is that I found objects so exactly as I had imagined them. . . . I was deceived only in its imaginary duration; for in [my dream] days and years and my entire life passed in an unchangeable tranquillity, whereas in fact all that lasted only for a moment. (CW5.90, OC1.107–8)

Petit and *maman* came to spend their summers in the country, at Les Charmettes near Chambéry. These were the "peaceful but fleeting[17] moments which have given me the right to say that I have lived." (CW5.189, OC1.225) So how did they end? What happened to this perfect union, the putting "our whole existence in common"? "It was not because of me," Rousseau tells us, "I

---

[17] Kelly tr., "quickly passing."

bear this consoling witness for myself. It was not because of her either, at least not because of her will. It was written that invincible natural disposition would soon take back its ascendancy." (CW5.186, OC1.222–3) Was the perfect union between *petit* and *maman* then contrary to nature? Or was it a failed attempt to transcend nature?

If we descend from these abstract musings to Rousseau's narrative of events, we learn that Jean-Jacques found himself ill, and imagined himself to have a polyp on the heart. Allegedly, a doctor in Montpellier had cured such an ailment; encouraged by Madame de Warens, Jean-Jacques set out to Montpellier in search of a similar cure. But as he remarks, "I did not need to go that far to find the doctor I needed" (CW5.208, OC1.248) – a certain Madame de Larnage, whom he, pretending to be an Englishman named Dudding, encountered en route at Moirans, who finally succeeded in making her desires known to him, and with whom he had the one truly and mutually passionate relationship of his life.

She was bound to Bourg-Saint-Andéol, and so they separated at Pont-Saint-Esprit, Jean-Jacques promising to visit her in the winter. But when the time came for him to leave Montpellier, a feeling of remorse returned, "so lively that, counterbalancing the love of pleasure, it put me in a condition to listen to reason alone." (CW5.217, OC1.259) And reason advised him that to continue to play an English gentleman without knowing a word of English was risky, that Madame de Larnage had a daughter, to whom his thoughts kept turning although he had not met her, and led him to wonder if he was to return "the mother's kindnesses" by "going to corrupt the daughter," and to reflect that his "mamma so good so generous . . . – already burdened with debts – was even more burdened with [his] foolish expenses," although he "was deceiving [her] so unworthily." (CW5.217, OC1.259–60) These edifying words of "reason alone" led him to hasten home to Chambéry rather than detouring to Bourg-Saint-Andéol, carefully advising Madame de Warens of the exact hour of his arrival.

> Thus I arrived exactly at the time. . . . I see no one in the courtyard, at the door, at the window. . . . The maid appeared surprised to see me. . . . I go upstairs, at last I see her, that dear Mamma so tenderly, so keenly, so purely loved; I run up to her, I throw myself at her feet. . . . A young man was with her. I knew him because I had already seen him in the house before my departure: but this time he appeared established there, indeed he was. In short I found my place taken. (CW5.218–9, OC1.261)

With the events described by Rousseau before us, we may return to the self. Rousseau had claimed that an "essential possession" united Jean-Jacques and *maman*. And now he says, "What a sudden and complete upheaval in all my being! . . . I – who since my childhood could see my existence only with hers – I saw myself alone for the first time. . . . Since that time my sensitive being has been half dead. . . . if sometimes an image of happiness still came into my desires, this happiness was no more my own."[18] (CW5.220, OC1.263) Jean-Jacques is no more his true self. And instructively, the few references to Madame de Warens that find their way into later books of the *Confessions* show that, in Rousseau's eyes, she too is no more herself. Twelve years pass, in which he makes only passing mention of "my poor mamma," and then: "I saw her again . . . in what a condition, my God! what degradation! what was left of her first virtue?" (CW5.328, OC1.391)

In a passage in the last *Promenade* that we shall discuss in detail in the final chapter, and that must remind us of Pygmalion's insistence that he no longer lives but through Galatea, Rousseau says, "I only lived in her[19] and for her." (CW8.89, OC1.1098) The loss of Madame de Warens was, for him, the loss of his true

---

[18] Kelly tr., "not the one suited to me."
[19] Butterworth omits the initial "her."

sentiment of existence. And in that sentiment there is no trace of the independent natural man. If Jean-Jacques is the man who is true to nature, he is not the man of nature that Rousseau describes in the *Discourse on Inequality*. He will become the solitary walker of the *Reveries*, but it would seem not by choice. For the man who is created in the *Confessions* is not a solitary but, in the deepest sense, a lover. He is totally dependent in his relation with Madame de Warens; she defines his role throughout, knowing that he "thought, felt, and breathed only through her." (CW5.169, OC1.201) But his dependence is not that of the citizen; Jean-Jacques comes to say not *aidons-nous* but *aimons-nous*. He lives in and for the loved one, as the citizen lives in and for the *patrie*, but the two lives originate in very different needs. May we then interpret Rousseau's life, as he constructs it in his confessional works, as an alternative to the lives ordained by the Tutor and the Legislator? The *Confessions* is "the first comparative base for the study of men"; is it an alternative to *Emile*? Is Madame de Warens, who gives Jean-Jacques his education in love, the true Tutor?

The last *Promenade* will help us answer these questions. But we should not overlook the final reference to *maman* in the *Confessions*.

My second loss, even more painful and much more irreparable, was that of the best of women and mothers who . . . left this Vale of tears to pass into the abode of the good, . . . Go, sweet and beneficent soul, . . . and prepare for your student the place he hopes to occupy one day near you. . . . Soon I also will cease to suffer, but if I believed I would not see her again in the other life, my weak imagination would not accept the idea of perfect happiness that I promise myself there. (CW5.519, OC1.619–20)

As Julie looked forward to eternal union with St. Preux, so Jean-Jacques looks forward to being again with his beloved *maman*.

The relationship between Jean-Jacques and *maman* is the central theme of the first part of the *Confessions*; its renewal in eternity is anticipated in the second part. Before concluding our discussion, we should look again to that second part, where Rousseau relates his two other principal relationships with a woman. One was his companion for over thirty years. The other was the "first and only one [i.e., love] in my whole life." (CW5.369, OC1.439) If, as I believe, Madame de Warens was the central figure in Rousseau's life, we need to examine the claims of these other women.

Rousseau met Thérèse Levasseur in 1745. She was a semiliterate serving maid, who was to become his companion, the mother of his children (all turned over to the foundlings' home for their upbringing), and eventually, in 1768, his wife. Rousseau tells us what we need to know about the basis of their relationship.

I have always regarded the day that united me with my Therese as the one that settled my moral being. I needed an attachment, because, in sum, the one that should have sufficed for me had been broken so cruelly. The thirst for happiness is never extinguished in the heart of man. Mamma was growing old and was demeaning herself. It had been proven to me that she could no longer be happy here below. It remained for me to seek a happiness that would be my own,[20] now that I had lost all hope of ever sharing hers. (CW5.347, OC1.413)

This is not quite the thought that he expressed after his rupture with *maman* – "if sometimes an image of happiness still came into my desires, this happiness was no more my own." But it makes clear the "second-best" character of his relation with Thérèse. As he goes on to say, "That is how the void in my heart was never very well filled, even in a sincere and reciprocal attachment into which I had put all the tenderness of this heart." (CW5.349, OC1.415)

"I have never felt the slightest spark of love for her." (CW5.348, OC1.414) This was neither sensuous nor platonic love. And there was certainly no union of souls, no existential identification.

---

[20] Kelly tr., "that would suit me."

Rousseau says, "I no more desired to possess her than Mme de Warens" (ibid.), but this comparison seems to confuse two senses of "possess." Since he continues immediately, "[T]he needs of the senses which I satisfied with her have been solely sexual," he can hardly be denying that he desired to possess Thérèse sexually, but it is precisely this that he did not desire with Madame de Warens. It seems most unlikely that he ever would have possessed *maman* sexually had she not decided on it. But if by "possess" he means essential possession, then as we have seen, he certainly wanted to possess Madame de Warens, and to do so fully and to be possessed by her, but not Thérèse. It is perhaps too harsh to say that she was simply a convenience for Rousseau, but he does say, "In Therese I found the supplement I needed." (CW5.278, OC1.332) A "supplement" does not determine one's sentiment of existence.

Thérèse is present in much of the second part of the *Confessions*, but is hardly a presence. With Élisabeth-Sophie-Françoise, Comtesse d'Houdetot, matters are almost reversed – although significantly present in but two of the six books in the second part, she is indeed a presence. For as Rousseau says, "this time it was love." (CW5.369, OC1.439) We should understand this claim primarily in terms of sensuous love. As Rousseau explicitly says, "And do not go on to imagine that my senses left me calm on this occasion, as they did with Therese and with Mamma." (CW5.374, OC1.445) When he would set out to visit her, passion would so overcome him that he would need to masturbate en route. And on arrival he would feel "the importunity of an inexhaustible and always useless vigor." (CW5.374–5, OC1.445) "Useless," because Sophie (as he called her) was the mistress of his friend St. Lambert, and while receptive to Rousseau's attentions, she drew the line at strict infidelity.[21]

---

[21] She was also married, but fidelity to her unloved husband was not the issue. Her concern was not to compromise her relationship with St. Lambert.

One beautiful moonlit night, Rousseau tells us, he and Sophie
walked in her garden to

a pretty grove adorned with a waterfall for which I had given her the
idea. . . . It was in this grove . . . that, in order to render the movements
of my heart, I found a language truly worthy of them. This was the first
and the only time in my life; but I was sublime. . . . What intoxicating
tears I shed on her knees! how I made her shed them in spite of herself!
Finally in an involuntary outburst she cried, 'No, never had a man been
so lovable, and never has a lover loved as you have! but your friend St.
Lambert is listening to you, and my heart cannot love twice.' I broke off,
sighing; I embraced her: what an embrace! But that was all. (CW5.373–4,
OC1.444)

And that, essentially, is all. Rousseau employs the language of
passion, but not that of identification. He is captured by his love
for Sophie, but he does not implicate his sense of self.

Rousseau does introduce the idea of possession in an unsent
letter to Sophie, in which he writes, "Did you not take possession
of me? You can never take that away, and because I belong to
you, in spite of myself and of yourself, let me at least be not
unworthy of belonging to you."[22] Sophie possesses Jean-Jacques,
but he does not possess her. One-sided possession is not a happy
situation for Rousseau; indeed, it is one of dependence, of lack
of freedom. It is not surprising that when he mentions her first
visit to him (it was with her second that his love began), he says
that it "unfortunately was not the last." (CW5.363, OC1.431)

The love affair, intense but unconsummated, lasted for only
a few months in 1757, with correspondence between the two
continuing into the following year. It was during this period that
Rousseau was completing *Julie,* and the two are not unconnected.
"I saw my Julie in Mme. d'Houdetot, and soon I no longer saw anything but Mme. d'Houdetot, but invested with all the perfections

---

[22] The translation is by Maurice Cranston, in the second volume of his biography of Rousseau, *The Noble Savage: Jean-Jacques Rousseau 1754–1762* (Chicago:
University of Chicago Press, 1991), 64.

with which I had just adorned the idol of my heart." (CW5.370, OC1.440) Julie is Jean-Jacques' ideal (in the person of St. Preux he is, after all, her lover and, we might say, acolyte). And so he attributes to Sophie her perfections, and makes the resulting image the object of his love. There is then an element of illusion in his love for Sophie. This would not surprise *Emile*'s Tutor, who would find his view of love at least partially confirmed.

If Julie affected the way in which Rousseau saw Sophie, it also seems that "some reminiscences of youth and Mme. d'Houdetot" entered into "the loves that I [Rousseau] felt and described" in *Julie.* (CW5.458, OC1.548) But as Philip Stewart notes in his introduction to *Julie,* "the novel was largely written before his passion for Sophie began." (CW6.xi) He acknowledges that "something of the experience found its way into the novel," but I think we may reasonably insist that the principal influence ran from Julie to Sophie, rather than vice versa. Rousseau had created Julie, and now in effect brought her to life for himself in the person of the Comtesse d'Houdetot. But if he is Pygmalion, his Galatea does not identify him as "Me again."

St. Preux's love for Julie was the defining and enduring center of his life. There is nothing comparable in Rousseau's love for Sophie. It was brief, passionate, and then it was over – Rousseau never suggests that he continued to love Sophie, or that he desired any renewal of their relationship, as he did with Madame de Warens. He does, however, make one significant comment on his love for Sophie that seems to echo a comment he makes about *maman.* He says, "I loved her too much to want to possess her."[23] (CW5.373, OC1.444) In discussing his lack of desire to possess Madame de Warens, he had said, "I loved her too much to covet her." (CW5.165, OC1.197) Since Rousseau distinguishes his love for Sophie from his care for *maman,* this parallel may

[23] It seems clear from the context that Rousseau is speaking of sexual possession – exactly what I insisted that he cannot be speaking of in denying the desire to possess Thérèse.

seem surprising. But I suggest that in fact the two remarks serve quite different purposes. His failure to covet Madame de Warens calls for explanation; he offers one that depends on the distinction between the love that is existential identification and the very different love that is desire for sexual possession. But his claim not to have wanted to possess Sophie is a plea for extenuation – having fallen in love with his friend's mistress, he wants to assure everyone that his affection for her held him back from any improper intent. One may or may not be convinced.

Rousseau's relationship with Sophie, like those with Mlle. Goton and Mme. de Larnage, belongs to the category of sensuous rather than platonic love. And it occupies a unique place in that category for Rousseau; it is the one instance in which he claimed to be truly in love with the object of his passion. But it is no more than that. Nothing in his account should lead us to equate it, in its significance for the making of Jean-Jacques, with his love for *maman.*

We are now ready for the reexamination of Rousseau's account of women that I promised in Chapter 2. There we found that woman is made "to be subjugated" (Bl.358, OC4.693) and that dependence on opinion, the primary cause of man's loss of freedom, and so "the grave of virtue among men," is nevertheless "its throne among women." (Bl.365, OC4.702–3) Thérèse, "the supplement I needed," and Sophie d'Houdetot, concerned to remain faithful in the eyes of her lover, are judged against Rousseau's standard of dependence. But Madame de Warens is not. To be sure, she needed the good opinion of the king of Sardinia to sustain her, but her personal life showed not the least sign of subservience. Her sexual activities proceeded without regard for convention or opinion. And in her relationship with Jean-Jacques, she was clearly the guiding force. As he admits, "I only lived in her[24] and for her." (CW8.89, OC1.1098)

---

[24] Butterworth tr. omits the initial "her."

Indeed, Madame de Warens could not have shaped Jean-Jacques had she been the creature of opinion whom Rousseau eulogizes in *Emile*. She must herself be free from ordinary human convention in order to enable Jean-Jacques to merge his existence with hers. So the woman who was at the center of Rousseau's life in no way displayed the supposed throne of feminine virtue.[25] What of Julie, his great creation? Recall her dying words to St. Preux, "The virtue that separated us on earth shall unite us in the eternal abode." (CW6.610, OC2.743) On earth, Julie's duty to her father and her husband, her dependence on their authority, reign supreme. But these deny her essential self. To regain it she must die, and pass into the realm where virtue is no longer linked to subjugation and opinion, but united with love and freedom. Julie reveals a view of women that both acknowledges and annuls Rousseau's insistence that opinion is the throne of a woman's virtue. In the eternal abode, virtue confers its blessing on the love that unites lovers into a single self. In believing that such a union awaited him, Rousseau transcended the separation of the sexes and the diminution of women that infected the teaching of Émile's Tutor.

Recall the distinction between love as one-sided possession of the beloved and love as essential union with the beloved. So long as a woman is the creature of opinion, she has no real self with which a lover could unite; she is fit only for being possessed.[26] There is a deep congruence between the accounts of female subordination and possessive love in *Emile*, but it is a congruence

[25] But Rousseau makes clear that Madame de Warens paid a cruel price for her lack of concern with opinion. Recall his words on seeing her in later years – "what degradation! what was left of her first virtue?" That "first virtue" freed her from the common fate of women, but she could not sustain it when fortune no longer smiled on her.

[26] For Rousseau, "possession" can mean one-sided "ownership" or "domination," of the female beloved by the male lover, contrasting with "essential possession" or "union" that mutually and reciprocally fuses the two lovers as a single self.

that denies and excludes St. Preux's impassioned insistence that lovers are not two but one. Rousseau's true doctrine of love may fit Julie and Madame de Warens, but only by undermining his account of women.

I have mentioned the division of the *Confessions* into two parts; this division is not unlike that between *Emile* and *Emile and Sophie*. Both the first part of the *Confessions* and *Emile* recount the story of a youth. Each ends when that youth enters the world – Émile as husband and father, Jean-Jacques as bound for Paris with his revolutionary system of musical notation. Each is the story, not simply of a youth, but of a youth being formed, and of the relationship between the youth and the person who forms him. At the end of each story, this relationship is left in suspense. I have examined the two relationships; presently I shall try to understand how they differ. But first, we should note the parallel between the second part of the *Confessions* and *Emile and Sophie*. Both recount the story of a man in a world centered on Paris, and of his relationships with the people in that world. In each the man comes to be exiled from that world, his fate undetermined.[27] Each is a story of the miseries undergone by the man. Each is a story in which the man becomes something other than he originally was, or seemed to be. That this is true of Émile is quite evident; in the next chapter I shall consider why it is also true of Jean-Jacques, and how we should understand his transformation.

How does Jean-Jacques' development differ from Émile's? I have already proposed an answer, in claiming that the key is the role played by love, or more precisely, the way in which the formation of Jean-Jacques' soul, and the determination of his sentiment of existence, is brought about when the liveliest of his desires, the diffuse desire to be loved, is made determinate

---

[27] Were *Emile and Sophie* finished, it might tell us Émile's fate. But if Rousseau had continued his *Confessions*, it might have told us his fate. And indeed, the *Reveries* does reveal it.

at the moment of his encounter with Madame de Warens. In addressing the magic words, *aimez-moi*, to her, the young Jean-Jacques opened himself to her influence. He admitted her into his soul, his self. She was the source of what he was becoming, and in identifying with her, in sharing with her an "essential possession which . . . depended on everything by which one is oneself" (CW5.186, OC1.222), Jean-Jacques could identify with his own becoming.

The Tutor controls Émile's development in ways of which Émile remains unaware. The education of nature, which the Tutor allegedly provides, is a process that remains opaque to the person being educated. Émile could not identify with it. No such alien process determined or changed the character of Jean-Jacques. Instead, his *maman* determined his development in ways with which he immediately identified. The education of love indeed depends on this – on the recognition that what one is becoming is one's true self. We should not read Rousseau's claim in the second *Dialogue*, that "[e]ducation has changed him [Jean-Jacques] very little" (CW1.107, OC1.799), as denying the all-embracing effects of the education of love. But before we can assess these effects, and consider the further changes that Jean-Jacques undergoes after leaving *maman*, we need to explore a very different dimension of Rousseau's life. We have discovered what he believed to be his true self; we must now examine his disguises.

6

Citizen of Geneva

"*Vitam impendere vero.*" The words are Juvenal's; the motto is Rousseau's.[1] "To devote one's life to the truth." My concern is with Rousseau's truth – with his attempt to discover his true self, and, in that self, "the first comparative base for the study of men." But we must examine this attempt with some caution. In his account to Malesherbes of his illumination, and his consequent career as an author, Rousseau comments, "Thus perhaps it is a hidden return of *amour propre* that made me choose and deserve my motto, and attached me so passionately to the truth, or to everything that I took for it."[2] (CW5.576, OC1.1136) His comment reveals a double hesitation. He suspects the presence in himself of *amour propre*, the force that leads to the externalization of the self, to taking one's sense of existence from the opinions of others. And this leads him to suspect his vision, to speak of it as "everything that I *took* for it [truth]" (my emphasis). In the preceding chapter we examined Rousseau's construction of himself as the man made for love – a construction that will culminate in his last promenade. We shall need to question whether

---

[1] Rousseau first proclaims this as his motto in the *Letter to d'Alembert*. See OC1.1788 (note 2 to page 1024) for a discussion of Rousseau's association of himself with truth.

[2] Kelly tr., "everything I have undertaken for it"; Fr. "*tout ce que j'ai pris pour elle.*"

this is Rousseau's truth. But we must also examine a second self-presentation that may seem equally to represent Rousseau's true nature – Citizen of Geneva.

I have already questioned Rousseau's identification of himself as the Citizen, suggesting that he could not have accepted the standard of citizenship that he develops in his political writings, and that he was at some level aware of this. I want now to try to confirm this suggestion, and thereby to complete the task of showing that making citizens is not, for Rousseau, a possible way to pass beyond our fallen condition – that his politics of redemption fails. And I want to argue that in representing himself as Citizen of Geneva, Rousseau is, albeit without direct acknowledgement, adopting a disguise, similar to the disguises he quite explicitly assumed earlier in his life. We need therefore to look at these other disguises. Once we understand their role, we shall be better placed to examine what Rousseau says, and does not say, both in the role of Citizen, and about that role.

Rousseau's first disguise is as a musician. To understand its significance we need some brief stage setting. Although he wrote several dramatic and musical works, only three were publicly performed during his lifetime.[3] *Pygmalion*, written in 1762, was staged by the Paris Opera ten years later, long after the events that will concern us. In October 1752 his ballet-opera, *The Village Soothsayer*, was performed before the king at Fontainebleau; two months later his comedy, *Narcissus*, was enacted by the Comédie française. Rousseau withdrew the play after its second performance, although he permitted its publication in the following year. The Comédie française would have accepted *Narcissus* into its repertory, but Fréron's comment, "Rousseau's desire was not to be applauded but to be hissed," is, as Jacques Scherer says in his introduction to the theatrical works in the *Oeuvres complètes*,

---

[3] I exclude here *Les Fêtes de Ramire*, which Rousseau was commissioned to adapt from a work by Voltaire and Rameau.

"the most penetrating remark."[4] But *The Village Soothsayer* was a different matter; successful before the king, it was received with acclaim in Paris and remained in the repertory of the Opera for many years. Rousseau himself remarked, "*The Village Soothsayer* put me completely in fashion, and soon there might not have been a man in Paris more sought after than I was." (CW5.309, OC1.369)

But if it made Rousseau fashionable, his opera also aroused envy among some of his contemporaries, and with that envy "a rumor . . . that I was not the Author." (CW5.321, OC1.383) Later this rumor was to become integral to Rousseau's conception of the universal plot against him, so that early in the first of the *Dialogues: Rousseau Judge of Jean-Jacques* we are informed by Rousseau's interlocutor, the Frenchman, that "it is a fact no one doubts any longer," since quite apart from the "well-attested plagiarisms" of which the opera is composed, Jean-Jacques "does not know music." (CW1.13–14, OC1.674–5)

Let us now go back from the 1770s, when Rousseau wrote the *Dialogues,* and from the 1750s, when *The Village Soothsayer* was first performed and doubts about its authorship were indeed heard, to 1732, when the young Jean-Jacques was with Madame de Warens in Annecy. Trying to find a suitable occupation for him, she had arranged that he would board and study music with the choirmaster. Unfortunately, the choirmaster had a falling out with his superiors and suddenly resolved to leave. Madame de Warens decided that Jean-Jacques should accompany him at least as far as Lyon. There the choirmaster had an epileptic fit, and Jean-Jacques shamelessly abandoned him. He returned to Annecy with thoughts only for his *maman*; he found her gone to Paris, leaving no explanation. Time passed; she did not return, and so it was decided that he should accompany Madame de Warens' maid back to her home in Fribourg. That

---

4 OC2.lxxxix, my trans.

accomplished, he found himself at loose ends. He made his way toward Lausanne, considering what to do.

Some months before, a young man, somewhat rakish in appearance and clearly straitened in circumstances, had arrived in Annecy, calling himself Venture de Villeneuve and claiming to be a musician from Paris. His charm and conversation soon made him the toast of the town, and Jean-Jacques was enthralled by him. And so as he entered Lausanne, Jean-Jacques' thoughts turned to Venture's entry into Annecy, and he decided to represent himself also as a musician from Paris, borrowing de Villeneuve for his own name and prefacing it with Vaussore, a kind of anagram of Rousseau. But unlike Venture, Vaussore de Villeneuve was a singing teacher who could not read music, and a composer who could not score a song. Undeterred, the so-called Vaussore undertook to compose a piece to be played at a concert in the home of the professor of law, and assumed the role of conductor. The resulting cacophony may be imagined, but the ending was in fact quite pretty, being the air of a well-known minuet that Jean-Jacques had learned from Venture.

Without of course denying that Rousseau's authorship of *The Village Soothsayer* was indeed called into question, I want to suggest that this incident in his past bears more than a casual relationship to the Frenchman's allegation, in the *Dialogues*, that the opera is composed of plagiarisms and that Jean-Jacques doesn't know music. What was false of Rousseau was indeed true of Vaussore. He was a plagiarist, and he did not know music.

Rousseau himself contrasts the whisperings of the audience in Lausanne with the very different exclamations with which *The Soothsayer* was greeted. But his contrast attests only to his own feelings in the two situations. It conceals more than it reveals. For what the accusations in the *Dialogues* show is surely his own doubt about his musical capability. Perhaps the composer of *The Soothsayer* is the old Vaussore? And perhaps, as with *Narcissus*, he is asking for the whisperings of ridicule rather than the exclamations of surprised pleasure.

Under a false name Rousseau played a false role. But I want to claim more – that by assuming a persona not his own, Rousseau enabled himself to play a false role. In his own person, he must devote his life to the truth – but as another person he is not under such a constraint. But when is Rousseau in his own person? Vaussore de Villeneuve is represented as a persona consciously assumed, but we should not suppose that Rousseau fully knew why he assumed it, or fully understood what he was licensing himself to do. And without this understanding, could he ever be sure that the pursuit of truth was indeed the end to which his actions were directed? Could he ever be sure of his real persona? And indeed, although he does not raise these questions in connection with his disguises, we shall find that he does seek explicitly to answer them in the *Reveries*. Rousseau's writings culminate in the quest for himself, for the assurance of his real persona. But that must await the final chapter.

Let us now turn to a second disguise – the Englishman Dudding, whom we encountered in the previous chapter, traveling from Moirans with Madame de Larnage. Vaussore represented himself as a musician, Dudding as a bashful lover. But where Vaussore showed his incompetence, Dudding, brought to the test, succeeded. To be sure, Madame de Larnage had to be a determined seductress, but at Valence Dudding finally recognized what she expected, and from then on he provided it. In his *Confessions*, Rousseau was to say that "I owe . . . to Madame de Larnage that I did not die without having known pleasure. . . . Oh, those three days! . . . I have not known their like since." (CW5.212–13, OC1.253–4)

If Vaussore made it possible for Jean-Jacques to be the musician that he was not, or rather was yet to be, Dudding made it possible for him to be the adventurer that he never was. Rousseau thought of himself as made for love, but not the kind of love Dudding enjoyed between Valence and Pont-Saint-Esprit. Indeed, Dudding may seem a strange interloper in that book of the *Confessions*, which begins with Jean-Jacques' removal with Madame de Warens to the country at Les Charmettes, "the short happiness of my life . . . the peaceful but fleeting[5] moments which have given me the right to say that I have lived." (CW5.189, OC1.225) Owing happiness and "having lived" to *maman* and Les Charmettes would not seem to leave room for owing pleasure to Madame de Larnage; Rousseau needs another persona to whom he can at least nominally assign the latter debt.

What, however, is of greatest import in Jean-Jacques' interlude in the role of an adventurer is the manner in which he abandoned it. In the preceding chapter I noted some of the considerations that he tells us ran through his mind – the possibility of being exposed as an impostor, the prospect of causing scandal by falling in love with the daughter, his continuing deception of his *maman*. Rarely has "listen[ing] to reason alone" (CW5.217, OC1.259) yielded such a wealth of advice as Jean-Jacques offered himself, culminating in the self-congratulatory recognition, as he passed the turning for Bourg-Saint-Andéol, that for the first time in his life, "I know how to prefer my duty to my pleasure." And "as soon as I had made my resolution I became another man, or rather I became again the one I had been before whom this moment of intoxication had made disappear." (CW5.217–18, OC1.260)

But it was not the intoxication of Madame de Larnage's advances that effected the transformation. Jean-Jacques had assumed the persona of Dudding from the outset. Again, I would suggest that he did not understand what he was licensing himself to do. In becoming Dudding, he was in effect making himself available to play the role of adventurer, should he be sufficiently prompted to do so. And prompting indeed there was. But when

5 Kelly tr., "quickly passing."

the prompting ended, and Dudding was cast off, Jean-Jacques could emerge purified, "thinking only of regulating my conduct upon the laws of virtue from now on, of dedicating myself without reserve to the service of the best of mothers, of swearing as much fidelity to her as I had attachment for her, and of no longer listening to any other love than that of my duties." (CW5.218, OC1.260) We should be wary of Rousseau's references to duties, for we shall later encounter his inability to accept their claims.

Dudding plays a clearly essential role in Rousseau's creation of Jean-Jacques as existing solely in and for his *maman*. For the dialogue enables Rousseau to represent the tie between the two as unbroken on Jean-Jacques' part, and so as essential to his nature. But it was surely no accident that when Jean-Jacques arrived in Chambéry he found his place taken. What Dudding concealed from him was that he had already left it.

As Vaussore and Dudding, Rousseau consciously presents himself as another person. With these as background, let us turn to Rousseau's presentation of himself as Citizen of Geneva. Once we grasp its significance, we can see that "Citizen of Geneva" is in fact another disguise. And understanding it as a disguise will cast a new light on the works that he authored as "Citizen of Geneva." It will show authorship as concealment. More particularly, it will put in question how these works relate to Rousseau's motto, "To devote one's life to the truth."

Rousseau's first uses of the words "Citizen of Geneva" are not innocuous, for they claim a status he did not possess at the time. Born to Genevan citizenship, he converted to Catholicism and so forfeited that status. He would not regain it until 1754, some four years after he had signed himself, in writing to Voltaire, "J. J. Rousseau, citoyen de Genève." The notes to the *Oeuvres complètes* suggest that he did this only to distinguish himself from another Rousseau, but his choice of "*citoyen*" is nevertheless worth noting, for he could have identified himself simply as "*de Genève.*" And some months later in 1750 the *Discourse on the Sciences and Arts* was published "Par un Citoyen de Genève," but without Rousseau's name. Several of his later writings then appeared by "Jean-Jacques [or J-J] Rousseau, Citoyen de Genève." Before cataloguing them we should ask why Rousseau takes up this identity when he does. And here we should recall his account of his walk to Vincennes, reading the *Mercury of France* en route, and coming upon the question of the Academy of Dijon. "At the moment of that reading I saw another universe and I became another man." (CW5.294, OC1.350–1) It was this other man who set out all that he "was able to retain of these crowds of great truths which illuminated" him under the tree where he let himself fall, in his "three principal writings," the two *Discourses* and the *Emile* – all attributed to the "Citizen of Geneva." (CW5.575, OC1.1136) In the quarter of an hour under one of the trees along the avenue, the man who had devoted his life to the truth believed that he had found his truths and been transformed, arising as the Citizen.

As we might expect, not only the *Discourse on the Origin of Inequality* (1755) and *Emile* (1762), but also the *Social Contract* (1762) identified the author as Citizen of Geneva. The *Discourse on Political Economy* appeared originally in Diderot's *Encyclopedia*, but was subsequently published separately (1756), with Rousseau identified as Citizen. The *Letter to d'Alembert* (1758), in which Rousseau criticized d'Alembert's proposal that a theater be established in Geneva, and the *Letter to Christophe de Beaumont* (1763), in which he defended his writings, and in particular *Emile*, against the criticisms of the archbishop of Paris, naturally included the identification. So did the *Extract of the Project of Perpetual Peace of the Abbé de Saint-Pierre*, which Rousseau published in 1761. In 1763 he renounced his Genevan citizenship, so that in the following year, when he published the *Letters Written from the Mountain* as a rejoinder to the attack on his religious and political writings by the Genevan Procurer-General Tronchin, he did not identify himself as Citizen, although it is worth noting that the title page included his motto, "*Vitam impendere vero.*"

But this is not the complete list. Two other works attributed to Rousseau as Citizen of Geneva appeared during his lifetime. And the first of these gives cause for more than a little puzzlement. *Julie* was published in 1761. Rousseau's name appeared, not as author, but in effect as editor – more specifically, the relevant part of the title page described the novel as "Letters Of Two Lovers, Inhabitants of a little Town at the foot of the Alps, Collected And Published By J. J. Rousseau." (OC2.1968, my trans.) The Second Preface to the work consists of a supposed dialogue between the editor (R.) and a man of letters (N.), and includes this exchange:

R. I am the Editor of this book, and I shall name myself as Editor.
N. You will name yourself? You?
R. Myself.
N. What! You will put your name on it?
R. Yes, Monsieur.
N. Your real name? *Jean-Jacques Rousseau*, in full?
R. *Jean-Jacques Rousseau* in full.
N. You wouldn't! What will people say?
R. Whatever they will. I put my name at the head of the collection, not to claim it as mine; but to answer for it. . . . .
N. On the title page of a love story we will read these words: *By J. J. ROUSSEAU, Citizen of Geneva!*
R. *Citizen of Geneva?* No, not that. I do not profane the name of my fatherland; I put it only on writings I believe will do it honor." (CW6.19–20, OC2.26–7)

The Second Preface was published separately from the novel. The author is identified as "*J. J. ROUSSEAU, Citoyen de Genève.*" Refusing explicitly to acknowledge (or equally to deny) his authorship of the novel, Rousseau nonetheless names himself author of the dialogue between himself, as its "editor," and the "man of letters." Withholding his status as Citizen of Geneva from any association with the novel, he nevertheless acknowledges it as author of the Preface.

Novels, like the theater, are not suited to Geneva, or at least to the Geneva of which Rousseau thought himself a citizen. The arts are not for the uncorrupted. But "[g]reat cities must have theaters; and corrupt peoples, Novels." (CW6.3, OC2.5) The language of love, in which *Julie* is written, can purify the hearts of men and women enslaved to the rule of social opinion, even if the purification extends only to their imagination. But it would undermine the rule of virtue. Julie meets her death in fulfilling her maternal duty. But she then embraces death as freeing her for a love that would deny the entire framework of duties – conjugal, maternal, and (we might say) seigneurial – that she has assumed as mistress of Clarens. As Clarens is the exemplar of Rousseau's claim that "[t]he family is . . . the first model of political societies" (CW4.132, OC3.352), to escape its duties is to escape the bonds of community. Julie's death expresses the transcendent power of the love that makes two persons one and closes them to the world; it does not convey a message suitable for Rousseau's virtuous citizens.

The novelist is thus not the Citizen of Geneva. But the citizen who responds to d'Alembert's proposal for a Genevan theater may also comment on the benefit of works of the imagination, as Rousseau does in the persons of the discussants in the Second Preface. *Julie* is a novel; the Second Preface is a disquisition about novels. There is no contradiction in Rousseau's insistence within the latter, which he writes in the capacity of citizen, that he does not edit the former in that same capacity.

One might suppose that after his renunciation of Genevan citizenship in 1763, Rousseau would not again identify himself in his authorial role as Citizen. But one late work did appear "by Jean-Jacques Rousseau, Citizen of Geneva." This is the brief story "*La Reine fantasque*" – "The Whimsical Queen" (or, since her name was Fantasque, "Queen Whimsy").[6] The exact date of this publication is uncertain; the year given on the title page is 1762, which of course would place it within the period of Rousseau's

---

[6] Translations from or concerning *La Reine fantasque* are my own.

citizenship, but for reasons discussed in the notes to the *Oeuvres complètes* (OC2.1987), the actual year must have been after 1769.

Although a story, "Queen Whimsy" is a work of political significance. It was written in 1756 and, long before Rousseau authorized its appearance, was published clandestinely in 1758 by Rousseau's enemies, who described it as a "*conte cacouac*," "*cacouac*" being a term of opprobrium applied to those involved in Diderot's *Encyclopedia*. It was then preceded by a caution, accusing the "*Cacouacs*" of wanting "to bury laws, morals, and religion in the same tomb," and claiming that "[s]tories like this . . . are traps set for humanity to part it from the sole path in which it can find rest and happiness," but are "so badly done that such stories bring with them their own refutation and condemnation." (OC2.1910) Rousseau would seem not to have known of this edition, and in later permitting the story to be published, he represented it simply as responding to a challenge "to make a tolerable and even cheerful story without intrigue, without love, without marriage, and without naughtiness." (OC2.1177)

I shall not attempt to recount the story here, save to say that the whimsies of the queen with regard to her son and daughter, which seem to threaten the good governance of the kingdom, are in the end prevented from having any adverse effects. The story endorses the king's "bizarre project of rending his subjects happy" (OC2.1179), and may well have seemed to Rousseau entirely innocuous in relation to his own political ideas. Had he known of its earlier unauthorized publication by his enemies, he might have wished, in subsequently authorizing its publication, to identify himself as "Citizen of Geneva" in order to deny, by implication, that the story was subversive of law, morals, and religion as he understood them. But since he lacked this knowledge, it may be that identifying Rousseau as Citizen was no more than the decision of the publisher, reflecting the political nature of the work. In any case, there seems no reason to read it as making a statement by Rousseau about himself.

Although canvassing Rousseau's authorial use of "Citizen of Geneva" offers some small surprises, we may conclude by accepting his claim in the Second Preface, that he uses it only for writings that he believes "will do it [Geneva] honor," these being the writings in which he develops both his critical and his constructive arguments about man and society. They are the writings appropriate to someone who accepts his ideal of citizenship. They are also the writings that emerge, directly or indirectly, from his illumination on the road to Vincennes. And so we should examine some of Rousseau's reflections on that illumination, and its effect on his character.

The *Discourse on the Sciences and Arts* was written in 1749. Rousseau tells us,

The following year 1750, when I was no longer thinking about my discourse, I learned that it had won the prize at Dijon. This news reawakened[7] all the ideas that had dictated it to me, animated them with a new strength, and finished setting into fermentation in my heart that first leaven of heroism and virtue which my Father and my fatherland and Plutarch had put there in my childhood. I no longer found anything great and beautiful but to be free and virtuous, above fortune and opinion, and to suffice to oneself. Although false shame and the fear of hisses kept me from behaving upon these principles at first[,] . . . I delayed executing this only for the amount of time it took for the contradictions to irritate it and render it triumphant. (CW5.298–9, OC1. 356)

Note first the core of what Rousseau claims here, that he found value only in freedom and virtue, in being above opinion, in sufficing for himself. In his first years in Paris, his sentiment of existence had come to depend on the opinions of his fellows; now he has reinternalized it, and thereby regained the condition of freedom that is incompatible with all dependence on others. To be sure, the transformation was not immediate; the opinions of others were not immediately silenced, as Rousseau's

---

7 Kelly tr., "reawoke."

reference to "the fear of hisses" makes clear. But transformation it was. Rousseau gave up a moderately comfortable position
with the wealthy Dupin family, where in addition to other tasks
he served as cashier to M. de Francueil, Mme. Dupin's stepson,
who was a receiver general of finances. In order to minimize his
dependence, he chose instead to live primarily on the earnings
he could derive from copying music. He reformed his sumptuary
habits, gave up fashionable dress (a matter facilitated by the theft
of "forty-two Shirts . . . of very fine cloth") (CW5.305, OC1.364),
and in general worked "to uproot from my heart everything that
still depended on the judgment of men." (CW5.306, OC1.364)

But there is a second matter to note in Rousseau's account
of his reawakening to freedom and virtue – its source. Rousseau
"was no longer thinking" about the *Discourse* and its ideas until
he received the news that it had won the prize. Not the illumination on the road to Vincennes itself, but the award of the
prize for the essay that embodied that illumination, "reawakened
all the ideas." But the award represents "the judgment of men."
Rousseau's assertion of independence, his reappropriation of his
sentiment of existence, was thus motivated not from within but
from his dependence on others – in this case, the members of
the Academy of Dijon. Rousseau shows no awareness of this. If
he had, he would have had to face a far deeper contradiction
than that between the way of life he had adopted in Paris and his
newfound principles. He would have had to face the dependence
that underlay his new life of independence.

A wider dependence on others becomes apparent when
Rousseau assesses, with the apparent wisdom of hindsight, the
intellectual and moral significance of his reawakening. He speaks
of being "thrown back without thinking about it into literature,
from which I believed I had departed forever, through that unfortunate discourse." (CW5.349, OC1.416) He tells us that "I no
longer saw anything but error and folly in the doctrine of our wise
men, anything but oppression and misery in our social order. In

the illusion of my foolish pride I believed I was made to dissipate all these impositions."[8] And he adds, "[J]udging that I needed to put my conduct into accord with my principles: in order to get a hearing, I took on the singular course which I have not been allowed to follow." His new words required new actions to confirm them. But if this was his reason for his changed conduct, then Rousseau treated it, not so much as expressing his newfound independence, but rather as enabling him to gain a hearing from his fellows.

Rousseau represented his reawakening as lasting until 1756, through the remainder of his years in Paris. During this period, he wrote his successful opera, *The Village Soothsayer*, and took a leading role in the extraordinary public controversy over the respective merits of Italian and French music, developing a theory of music that denied any merit whatsoever to the French. He responded for a second time to the announcement of an essay competition by the Academy of Dijon with his *Discourse on the Origin of Inequality*. He journeyed to Geneva in 1754, where he was received back into the Protestant faith and readmitted to citizenship, bringing his legal status into line with his authorial invocations.

Rousseau sketches the man he came to be after he took on the task of dissipating the folly of the wise and the oppressions of society. "Until then," he tells us,

I had been good; from then on I became virtuous, or at least intoxicated with virtue. . . . I put on no act;[9] I in fact became what I appeared to be, and during the period of at least four years that this effervescence lasted in all its force, between Heaven and myself there was nothing great and beautiful that could enter into the heart of a man of which I was not capable. . . . I was truly transformed; my friends, my acquaintances no

---

[8] Rousseau's term is "*prestiges*," translated by Kelly as "illusions." This is unhelpful, since Kelly has used "illusion" to translate Rousseau's term "*illusion*" earlier in the sentence.

[9] Kelly tr., "I play acted nothing."

longer recognized me. . . . All Paris repeated the bitter and mordant sarcasms of this same man who two years before and ten years afterward could never find what he wanted to say, or the word he ought to use. Look for the condition in the world most contrary to my natural disposition; this one will be found. Recall those short moments of my life when I became another person,[10] and ceased to be me; the time about which I am speaking is one of them; but instead of lasting six days, six weeks, it lasted almost six years, and would perhaps still be lasting, if it were not for the particular circumstances that made it cease, and returned me to nature above which I had wanted to raise myself." (CW5.350, OC1.416–7)

I want to focus on six brief passages from Rousseau's account of his transformation: (i) "I put on no act" (*"Je ne jouai rien"*); (ii) "I in fact became what I appeared to be"; (iii) "I was truly transformed"; (iv) "Look for the condition in the world most contrary to my natural disposition; this one will be found"; (v) "I became another person, and ceased to be me"; (vi) ". . . circumstances . . . returned me to nature above which I had wanted to raise myself."

The first passage is a declaration of sincerity. Rousseau abandoned all pretence of fashion, adopted an individual and peculiar style of dress, ignored the customary niceties and taboos of polite conversation. He wanted to refute the charge that he was merely playacting. He wanted to insist that his behavior reflected his beliefs. He had of course already admitted that he was the victim of an illusion caused by "foolish pride." And more worryingly, we have found that opinion played a role in motivating this behavior. But this affects the significance to be placed on his transformation rather than its overt sincerity.

The second passage emphasizes the depth of his transformation. His new mode of behavior determined his appearance, his being in the world or his being-for-others. But he wanted to insist that he came to be as he appeared, that his

---

[10] Kelly tr., "someone else."

being-for-himself came to be the same as his being-for-others. How should we interpret this? In the *Discourse on the Origin of Inequality*, to be as one appears to others is at the core of our fallen condition. But Rousseau is not representing himself as fallen. Social beings, according to Rousseau, exist only in their appearance – they have no identity beyond their being-for-others. Rousseau is instead insisting on his own transparency – nothing is concealed in his being-for-others. But at the same time he recognized that the self revealed by his appearance is not his original self; it is the product of a transformation. And this of course is what he claimed in (iii). He did not appear as the self he was originally, but as the self he had become through the transformation that was shaped under the tree on the road to Vincennes, and spurred by the news from Dijon.

We come now to the heart of Rousseau's account – the recognition that the effect of his transformation was to make him another person, of a character quite opposed to his original nature (iv), so that he was no longer himself (v). Rousseau has emphasized his sincerity; what he must acknowledge is that the sincerity nevertheless expressed an illusion. The identity he has acquired is in some sense a false identity, an identity expressive of a character quite opposed to his own, a self that was not his self. Rousseau's claims about his nature may appear contradictory, but we may best interpret them as revealing his not-quite-explicit recognition of an inner conflict between the person he sincerely took himself to have become, and the very different self that he in fact continued to be. To this extent his enemies were right in detecting something false in Rousseau's appearance. This is why his suspiciousness of his enemies was "guilty."[11] Although he was not, as they thought, playing a false part, he was living a false identity.

[11] Recall the reference to Jean-Jacques' "guilty suspiciousness" in the *Dialogues*. (CW1.40, OC1.711); Chapter 2 *supra*.

And so he claimed that circumstances restored him to nature (vi). We may relate his wanting to raise himself above nature to the illusion of his foolish pride. He did not knowingly accept a false understanding of himself, but nevertheless his pride led him astray from the demand of his motto, to devote one's life to the truth. And this same pride led him to consider himself born to clear away the folly of the wise and the oppressions of the social order – to speak with the voice of the Citizen of Geneva.

Rousseau assumes the mantle of Citizen of Geneva at the time of his transformation, and having donned this mantle, he preaches the views that his transformation has led him to espouse. He acknowledges that in this transformation, he becomes other than himself. But is this sufficient for us to equate the false other with the Citizen – to treat *assuming the mantle* of Citizen as equivalent to *taking on the guise* of Citizen? Rousseau describes his transformation, but he gives it no name, nothing corresponding to Vaussore or Dudding.

Rousseau of course discusses his readmission to Genevan citizenship in the *Confessions*. But his only reference to his assumption of the title of Citizen is not in this connection; it appears instead in relation to the *Discourse on Inequality*. "The only advantage this work procured me – aside from the one of having satisfied my heart – was the title of Citizen which was given to me by my friends, then by the public after their example, and which I later on lost[12] for having deserved it too well." (CW5.332, OC1.395) Although he occasionally refers to himself as Citizen, he never speaks, in the *Confessions*, of his authorial use of the title Citizen of Geneva.

Rousseau's silence is not, I think, an obstacle to treating the assumption of the mantle of Citizen as taking on a guise, given

---

[12] Does Rousseau mean that the term ceased to be applied to him by his friends and the public? Or does he, more plausibly, mean that in the aftermath of his condemnation by Geneva, he renounced the status of citizen in 1763?

that he does explicitly insist that in the aftermath of his illumination on the road to Vincennes he becomes another person and ceases to be himself, and given the hardly contestable observation that the authorial voice he employs as this other person is that of the Citizen. But there is an apparent obstacle, which is that he continues to employ this voice after he has returned to nature and ceased being other than himself. "This change [to his old self] began as soon as I had left Paris, and the spectacle of the big City's vices ceased to nourish the indignation it had inspired in me. . . . without anyone noticing it, . . . I again became fearful, accommodating, timid, in a word the same Jean-Jacques I had been before." (CW5.350, OC1.417)

Thus we face this simple chronological problem. According to his own claims, Rousseau began to be restored to himself when he left Paris, which took place in April 1756. Furthermore, he speaks of his transformation into someone other than himself as lasting almost six years, and he could hardly have supposed that it commenced later than February 1751, when he resigned his position with the Dupins. But he continued to publish as Citizen of Geneva until March 1763. If his guise, whatever it was, ceased in 1756, and if he continued to write as the Citizen for seven more years, then it would seem that we may not identify the guise with the mantle of the Citizen.

There is a counter to this objection, and it is perhaps best conveyed by the concluding words of a letter from Diderot to Rousseau at the Hermitage, where he had taken up residence after leaving Paris. (Rousseau quotes from this letter in the *Confessions*, but not its conclusion.) "Adieu, Citizen – and yet a hermit makes a very peculiar citizen."[13] From the publication of the first *Discourse* and his decision to live as a music copyist until he left Paris, Rousseau's assumption of the mantle of Citizen appeared

---

[13] Quoted in Maurice Cranston, *The Noble Savage: Jean-Jacques Rousseau 1754–1762* (Chicago: University of Chicago Press, 1991), 47.

plausible. He went to Geneva to bring his real status into conformity with the title to which he had laid claim, and, as he tells us
in his account of his stay there, "I thought of returning to Paris
only to dissolve my household, put my little affairs in proper
order, place Mme. le Vasseur and her husband [his companion
Thérèse's parents] or provide for their subsistence, and come
back with Therese to establish myself at Geneva for the remainder of my days." (CW5.330, OC1.393) Rousseau was acting the
part he had taken for himself. We may see his reincorporation
among the citizenry of Geneva, with its necessary accompani-
ment of his readmission to the Protestant communion, and his
apparent intention to resettle in Geneva, as integral to his transformation.

But he never set foot in Geneva again. He did in time leave
Paris, but for the Hermitage rather than Geneva. His choice is
deliberate; he tells us that "[r]enouncing the stay in my fatherland I resolved, I promised to live in the Hermitage" (CW5.332,
OC1.396), the promise being made to its owner, Mme. d'Epinay,
who pressed it upon him. He remarks that Voltaire's decision
to settle near Geneva influenced him against return, since he
saw Voltaire as sure to exercise a corrupting influence on his
native city.[14] And he excuses himself from taking on the task of
combatting Voltaire, saying that to do so he "would have to bat-
tle ceaselessly" and would prove "an unbearable pedant," unless
he allowed himself to be "a lax and bad citizen." (CW5.333,
OC1.396) It is evident that Rousseau had come to have no stom-
ach for what he recognized as the demands that real citizenship
would put upon him. Contrast this with Rousseau's account of his
transformed self – "In the illusion of my foolish pride I believed

---

[14] In his biography, Cranston casts doubt on Voltaire's presence as Rousseau's
reason. (*The Noble Savage*, 10) At the time he left Paris, Rousseau did not
hold the very negative view of Voltaire that he certainly embraced when he
wrote the *Confessions*. But my concern is with the person constructed in the
Confessions, whether or not this person is the same as the man himself.

I was made to dissipate all these impositions." (CW5.349, OC 1.416)

Once at the Hermitage, Rousseau showed not the slightest yearning to reside in or even to visit his *patrie*. Indeed, when Mme. d'Epinay asked him to accompany her to Geneva, where she wished to consult the doctor Tronchin, he refused. He had strong personal reasons for doing so, although he only alludes to them in the *Confessions*, but what is important for our purpose is that his reasons were strictly personal. The connection between Geneva and Rousseau as Citizen had been abandoned.[15] And so I want to argue that Rousseau was right to think that he had become a different man in the aftermath of his illumination, a man whose trajectory led him to be the Citizen whose task it was to expose the injustice of the existing social order, but that after his departure from Paris, he lost the zeal of that different man. What requires explanation is not the proposal to equate this different man with the Citizen of Geneva, but rather Rousseau's continued authorial invocation of the Citizen after he had returned to the nature "above which [he] had wanted to raise [himself]."

The explanation emerges from reflection on the post-1756 works that received this invocation. The most important, *Emile* and the *Social Contract*, represent the working out of ideas that derived from the illumination on the road to Vincennes, and were among the projects that Rousseau took with him when he left Paris for the Hermitage.[16] The *Extract of the Project of Perpetual*

---

[15] As Cranston notes, "when any scheme was suggested to Rousseau that might facilitate his return to Geneva, he immediately found fault with it." (*The Noble Savage*, 45) However, when Rousseau was forced to leave France and chose to seek asylum in Switzerland, he did involve himself extensively in Genevan politics, although this involvement is largely ignored in the self-construction of the *Confessions*.

[16] In the case of the *Social Contract*, the project was, of course, the study of political institutions, which Rousseau abandoned, keeping only the *Social Contract* as the one completed part.

Peace of the Abbé de Saint-Pierre was also among these projects. The *Letter to d'Alembert* was specifically concerned with Geneva, and the *Letter to Beaumont* was a response to criticisms of his writings and especially of *Emile*. Rousseau insisted that "if one wants to dedicate books to the true good of the fatherland, one must not compose them in its bosom." (CW5.341, OC1.406) Thus he could represent these writings to himself, and so to the world, as coming from the Citizen, even if he was "a very peculiar citizen."

But Rousseau himself notes a difference in tone between these works and the writings he published while still in Paris and caught up in the effervescence that made him a changed man. Commenting on the *Letter to d'Alembert*, the first of his post-Paris publications, he notes, "Ill humor did prevail in all the writings I had done at Paris: it no longer reigned in the first one I had done in the country." (CW5.420, OC1.502) And he continues, "That remark was decisive for those who know how to observe. They saw that I had returned into my element."[17] Elsewhere in the *Confessions*, he speaks of both "the bile" (CW5.309, OC1.368) and the "truly celestial fire" (CW5.350, OC1.416) that were present in his first Parisian writings; his post-Parisian works, by contrast, "breathed a gentleness of soul" (CW5.420, OC1.503) that surely excludes bile and celestial fire alike.

Rousseau's reversion to his old self was emotional and existential, rather than in the narrow sense intellectual. And so he continued to write, and no doubt to think of himself, as the Citizen of Geneva. But he came to live as, and in the person of, a solitary, longing for the merging of souls that he had once enjoyed with Madame de Warens, but finding instead that "the void in [his] heart was never very well filled." (CW5.349, OC1.415)

---

[17] Commenting on this passage, the editors of the *Oeuvres complètes* say, "Quickly enough, the 'citizen' realized that the *Letter* made him 'return into [his] element'." (OC1.1518, my trans.) This comment conveys exactly my contention that in returning to the country, the "citizen" has ceased to be the Citizen.

Rousseau's devotion to truth did not prevent him from assuming two significant disguises – the musician Vaussore de Villeneuve, at a time when he lacked competence in music, and the English traveler and man of the world Dudding, so that he might enjoy sexual pleasure. It also did not prevent him from assuming the guise of Citizen, so that he might deliver his message of alienation and redemption. His first disguises deceived others, but they also deceived him insofar as he remained unaware of their effect in enabling him to attempt what in his own person he could not. Indeed, they permitted a deceit that his own dedication to truth would have forbidden. The same seems to me true of his disguise as Citizen. As Vaussore knew no music and Dudding no English, so the Citizen knew no redemption.

Although Rousseau claimed to have been returned to nature, almost immediately he revised this claim. "If the revolution had done nothing but return me to myself and stop there, all would have been well; but unfortunately it went farther and carried me away rapidly to the other extreme. From that time my soul has been in motion and has no longer done anything but pass through the line of rest and its ever renewed oscillations have never allowed it to stay there." (CW5.351, OC1.417) And indeed, the second part of the *Confessions* is the account of a soul in turmoil. In the next chapter I shall consider what Rousseau said in the *Reveries* about himself as a member of society, which will confirm my interpretation of the Citizen as disguise. But here we should consider that other extreme to which Rousseau was carried – neither the lover nor the citizen, but the paranoid who saw himself society's victim. Does it reveal or conceal a truth about Rousseau?

Let us then look at the second part of the *Confessions* as a whole. We should keep in mind those passages, discussed in the preceding chapter, that relate to Madame de Warens, Thérèse, and Sophie, and which, I argued, do not represent any transformation or alteration of Rousseau's nature. Here I have been examining only the few pages in which Rousseau does discuss his transformation into another self – a self that I have identified with the Citizen of Geneva. But Rousseau pays little overt attention to the Citizen. Equally, he pays little attention to the man who left the cocoon at Chambéry to make his way in Parisian society. In the *Epistle to Parisot*, we find this man hoping to make his way in the world, accepting the graces of civilization and indeed "the attractions of an opulent life" (OC2.1141, my trans.), while rejecting "debauch and excess." And that young man appeals to the correction of his manners brought about by his benefactress, "that tender mother." (OC2.1139, my trans.) By contrast, early in the seventh book of the *Confessions* Rousseau says: "What a different picture I will soon have to develop! Fate, which favored my inclinations for thirty years, contradicted them for another thirty." (CW5.233, OC1.277) At the beginning of the next, eighth book, he writes, "I was obliged to make a pause at the end of the preceding Book. With this one begins the long chain of my misfortunes in its first origin." (CW5.293, OC1.349) And the book concludes, "[B]ut since in the end my name must live, I ought to try to transmit along with it the remembrance of the unfortunate man who bore it, as it was really, and not as unjust enemies work without respite to depict it." (CW5.336, OC1.400)

In the first paragraph of the tenth book, Rousseau tells us,

Having returned from the chimeras of friendship, detached from everything that had made me love life, I no longer saw anything in it that could make it pleasant for me: I no longer saw anything in it but evils and miseries that prevented me from enjoying myself. I aspired to the moment of being free and escaping my enemies. But let us take up the thread of events again. (CW5.410, OC1.489)

And the book ends,

I can no longer proceed except in the track of my remembrances: but they are such in this cruel epoch, and the strong impression of it has remained with me so well, that, lost in the immense sea of my misfortunes, I cannot forget the details of my first shipwreck, although its consequences no longer offer me anything but confused remembrances. Thus I can still proceed in the following book with enough assurance. If I go farther, it will no longer be except by groping. (CW5.455, OC1.544)

And when he does go farther, in the twelfth and last book, he writes, "Here begins the work of darkness in which I have found myself enshrouded for the past eight years without having been able to penetrate its frightening obscurity no matter what I might try to do about it." (CW5.493, OC1.589) The book concludes with his departure from Bienne, having been expelled from all Bernese territory, believing himself bound for Berlin, but actually destined to England, and to his famous quarrel with David Hume. Rousseau appends an account of reading his *Confessions*, declaring "I have told the truth," claiming that anyone who examines "my natural disposition, my character, my morals, my inclinations, my pleasures, my habits, and will be capable of believing that I am a dishonest man, is himself a man fit to be stifled." (CW5.549–50, OC1. 656) The reading was greeted, we are told, with silence.

What are we to make of this litany of woes? We may understand it as confession, as Rousseau's plea before his judge, but as anthropological document? As I noted in the second chapter, Rousseau was regarded as a man of dangerous views by defenders of the established order, whether in Catholic, cosmopolitan, authoritarian Paris or in Protestant, insular, theocratic Geneva. His religious and political opinions were equally at odds with those of his sometime associates, the atheistic or deistic advocates of scientific and economic advancement. Real persecution fueled the increasing paranoia recorded in the second part of the *Confessions*. Why is there more to be said?

Let us turn again to the second *Dialogue*, and to the passage that I discussed in the third chapter, in which the character

Rousseau says of Jean-Jacques, "He is everything to himself; he is also everything to them. For as for them, they are nothing either to him or to themselves." (CW1.155, OC1.860) It is instructive that Rousseau's remarks begin with a reference to the *Confessions* as "that work unique among men." Jean-Jacques is different; he is, as Rousseau described him earlier in the *Dialogue*, "what nature made him." (CW1.107, OC1.799) He is everything for himself, the center of his own existence. But he is also the center of his enemies' existence. Unable to sense their existence in themselves, to be their own centers, they exist in him, but in their negation of him. If they were to recognize his true self, they would also recognize their own falsity. But "as long as J. J. is miserable, they need no other happiness." (CW1.155, OC1.860) So what can the natural man be in the social world but the object of universal persecution? For he reveals the emptiness, the inauthenticity of social existence. Jean-Jacques can be the person he claims to be, only in becoming the object of universal execration.

But I have questioned whether the man whose writings – *Emile*, the *Social Contract* – invited persecution is indeed the person he claims to be. Rousseau put on the mantle of Citizen of Geneva, but the role he assigns to the citizen is one he never played. Within two months of being restored to Genevan citizenship he left the city, never to return. Indeed, as we shall see in the next chapter, the role of citizen was one he recognized that he never could have played. And he could not have played it because it would have required him to deny his real self, to deny the nature that he was never truly able to abandon, despite his claims to transformation. Yet he spoke as the Citizen. There may, then, have been two rather different thoughts struggling in Rousseau's mind. "If I am indeed as nature made me, then I am, inevitably but undeservedly, the object of persecution by those who are as society has deformed them." "If I am not the Citizen, but only appear to be, then I am, deservedly, the object of persecution by those who recognize my inauthenticity."[18] These thoughts converge in the representation of Jean-Jacques as the victim of persecution. In this respect they reinforce each other. But any attempt to entertain them simultaneously would induce the most severe cognitive dissonance. Rousseau suppressed the second. In the *Confessions* he treated his readmission to Genevan citizenship as the result of "abandon[ing himself] entirely to patriotic zeal" (CW5.329, OC1.392) because of the acclaim occasioned by his visit. He made no mention of his prior authorial invocation of the title, or his subsequent use of it. Its inadequately acknowledged presence would help to explain why he remained in a state of darkness about himself, a state that he externalized in the universal plot that he found not only incomprehensible, but indiscernible.

The two parts of the *Confessions* provide us with complementary portraits. In the first, we see how Jean-Jacques is formed through his relationship with Madame de Warens, how he achieves – and loses – the existential identification with her in which he senses his existence only in common with hers. We come to understand the deep significance of *aimez-moi*, of the demand to be loved, in the formation of the truly natural man. And in the second part, we see how Jean-Jacques comes to be regarded in the world of denatured, disfigured social men. But we also find, in this second part, a complicating feature of the portrait – his alleged transformation. When he lost the enthusiasm that led him to think himself another man, he did not return to the Jean-Jacques of the years at Chambéry, but became an unstable paranoid. Only in the *Reveries*, when he acknowledged his unfitness for social life, did he reach that point in his self-examination in which he was able fully to return to his earlier self-understanding, as the man shaped by the demand for love.

[18] Recall again the "guilty suspiciousness" attributed to Jean-Jacques by the Frenchman in the first *Dialogue*. (CW1.40, OC1.711)

7

The Last Promenade

"I am now alone on earth, no longer having any brother, neighbor, friend, or society other than myself. The most sociable and the most loving of humans has been proscribed from society by a unanimous agreement." (CW8.3, OC1.995) In the *Discourse on the Origin of Inequality*, Rousseau read the history of humankind, beginning in solitude with society gradually emerging. Our history is that of a solitary creature becoming social. Now, in the first words of the *Reveries of the Solitary Walker*, Rousseau reads his own history as that of a social creature becoming once more solitary, writing "my reveries only for myself." (CW8.8, OC1.1001) "But I, detached from them [everyone] and from everything, what am I myself?[1] That is what remains for me to seek." (CW8.3, OC1.995) From reading the history of humankind in nature to applying the barometer to his soul – this is Rousseau's journey, and this is the man he is – the man whose final question is "what am I myself?" And so in this final chapter we shall accompany him on the ten promenades that compose the *Reveries*, seeking, with him, the answer to his question.

Rousseau is writing only for himself. The reading that reflexively concluded the *Confessions* contrasts with the writing that

---

[1] Butterworth tr. omits "myself"; Fr. "*que suis-je moi-même?*" Further notes omit translator's name.

reflexively opens the *Reveries*. The reading concluded in silence. Rousseau now accepts that silence; he no longer tries to speak across the gap that he believes divides him from his fellows. But we must ask whether this gap is part of his answer to what he is. For before we begin our final journey with him, we should take note of a deeply illuminating comment from the *Dialogues* about the solitary Jean-Jacques. The comment is made by the character Rousseau, who says, "But I also know that absolute solitude is a state that is sad and contrary to nature: affectionate feelings nourish the soul, communication of ideas enlivens the mind. Our sweetest existence is relative and collective, and our true *self* is not entirely within us." (CW1.118, OC1.813) Absolute solitude is man's natural condition, according to the writer of the *Discourse on Inequality*. If this solitude is contrary to nature, then we must understand it as that second nature that humans acquire through their perfectibility. Man's original sentiment of existence is entirely within himself. If this is not the sense of the true self, and if our perfected self exists in relation to others, then what is the nature of this relationship? Is it the relationship originally expressed by *aidez-moi*, transformed into the *aidons-nous* of ideal citizens? Or is it the relationship expressed by *aimez-moi*, transformed so that there is neither "*moi*" nor "*toi*" – ideal lovers who "are no longer two, they are one"? (CW6.555, OC2.676) We shall need to keep this important comment in mind as we accompany the solitary walker, asking whether Rousseau's self-portrait in the *Reveries* contradicts or confirms the claim that "[o]ur sweetest existence is relative and collective."

In the first promenade Rousseau tells us – or more accurately, tells himself – that "[n]ot quite two months ago, complete calm was reestablished in my heart." (CW8.5, OC1 997) If the text nevertheless betrays his former agitation, we may see its breaking waves as the remains of a storm now past, the water not yet still, the reflections only gradually becoming clear. Why calm has returned to him is not revealed; he speaks of "[a]n event as sad as it was unforeseen" that "finally . . . erased" all hope and left him utterly resigned, but he does not identify this event. Some critics have argued, although more have denied, that it is the event that he describes in the second of the *Reveries*, an autumn walk in the countryside near Paris. Whether or not the events are the same, the walk offers the first of Rousseau's reflections.

Returning on the road leading down from Ménilmontant, Rousseau was bowled over by a Great Dane, which was running at full tilt ahead of a carriage. He lost consciousness. On coming to, he became aware of the sky, the stars beginning to appear in the advancing night, some foliage.

I was born into life at that instant, and it seemed to me that I filled all the objects I perceived with my frail existence. Entirely absorbed in the present moment, I remembered nothing; I had no distinct notion of my person. . . . I felt a rapturous calm in my whole being; and each time I remember it, I find nothing comparable to it in all the activity of known pleasures. (CW8.12, OC1.1005)

"What am I myself?" In this moment of birth Rousseau is nothing himself; he has no existence in time, no existence in the present apart from the objects of his perception. Whether the "complete calm" reestablished in his heart is or is not the "rapturous calm" felt in all his being, we may take this moment as the real beginning of the *Reveries*, in which Rousseau finds himself with an almost blank slate – a single feeling of calm, a perception of sky, stars, and foliage. Whatever he has been, he seems now free to create himself anew, to answer his question unburdened by – though not unmindful of – the past. But the response to his accident, among his acquaintances and among the public, reawakened his paranoia. Much of the reaction seems innocent enough, although rumors of his death from the fall did lead to obituaries that spoke of Rousseau's abuse of his talents, but all was fuel for his fire. And he no longer found only human malevolence working against him. Since "all the acts of will, all the unlucky events, fortune and all its revolutions have made firm the work of men" (CW8.15, OC1.1010), he saw Heaven's eternal decree in the universal conspiracy, and this brought him consolation, with the belief that "everything must return to order, and my turn will come sooner or later." (CW8.16, OC1.1010) Once again calm is restored.

In the next two promenades Rousseau turns to self-examination. He considers and rejects Solon's motto, "I continue to learn while growing old" (CW8.17, OC1.1011), preferring to reaffirm the faith he expressed in the person of the Savoyard vicar in *Emile*, and trusting in the care with which he conducted his enquiries at a time when his powers of reasoning were at their height. The Savoyard vicar, who provides a model of the instruction Émile should receive in matters of religion, plays a role not open to the Tutor or indeed to Rousseau himself, since their powers are strictly secular. Faith enters into the making of a man, or a citizen, or Jean-Jacques himself. If one is to believe in the moral order of the universe, and embrace one's place in that order, then Rousseau is convinced that one must accept "a powerful, intelligent, beneficent, foresighted, and providential Divinity; the afterlife; the happiness of the just; the punishment of the wicked." (CW4.223, OC3.468) The citizen must accept "the sanctity of the social Contract and the Laws," and all must reject intolerance. These are the dogmas of the civic religion Rousseau sketches in the *Social Contract*. They are deeply important to him, but in part because of their importance, we may treat them as common elements in all of his attempts to find a way to redeem our fallen condition, present in his understanding both of himself and of humankind. Although they may occasion controversy with his contemporaries, whether atheists or Christians, they do not occasion controversy within his own thought. And so I have passed over the vicar's role in *Emile*, and the place of civic religion in the good society, and shall now pass over this part of Rousseau's self-examination in the *Reveries*. Its presence licenses Rousseau to continue to embrace his metaphysics, as it were – the framework of things transcending our earthly condition that permit us to seek to live within a moral order. In asking "What am I myself?" he may continue to embrace the faith in which he has lived. And so he turns to an examination of truth in the fourth promenade, for it is tied to the motto that we have already encountered, *Vitam impendere vero,* "to devote one's life to the truth."

Rousseau's reflection arises when he finds in a volume of the Abbé Rosier sent him by the author, the written inscription "*Vitam vero impendenti, Rosier,*" which he interprets as a cruel thrust at himself. But he focuses on the text and not the intent, and devotes his walk to "examining myself on lying and I came to it quite confirmed in the . . . opinion that the 'know thyself' of the temple of Delphi was not as easy a maxim to follow as I had believed in my *Confessions.*" (CW8.28, OC1.1024)

He begins by considering what may be the worst of his actual lies – his accusation, when a youth in service, of a young serving girl for stealing a ribbon that he had in fact taken himself. And he credits this event with giving him a horror of falsehood that was at the root of his determination to devote his life to the truth. But he sees that the task is less easy or straightforward than it may appear, acknowledging "the number of things of my own invention I recalled having passed off as true at the same time that, inwardly proud of my love for truth, I was sacrificing my security, my interests, and myself to it with an impartiality of which I know no other example among human beings." (CW8.29, OC1.1025) Rousseau finds himself puzzled by this seeming contradiction in his behavior, and embarks on a somewhat tortuous inquiry that finally leads to an apparent conclusion: "The difference . . . between my *truthful* man and the other man [i.e., the man taken for truthful by the world] is that the world's is very rigorously faithful to every truth which costs him nothing, but not beyond that, whereas mine never serves it so faithfully as when it is necessary to sacrifice himself for it." (CW8.34, OC1.1031) But Rousseau's truthful man embodies the puzzle he was intended to resolve; how can he be truly devoted to truth so that he sacrifices himself for it, and yet careless of truth when it is, at least ostensibly, of no concern?

Rousseau ascribes his lapses from truth as owing to shame or timidity. But something deeper seems at stake, as his next memory reveals. Asked by a young and pregnant woman at dinner if he had any children, he replied that he "had not had this good fortune" (CW8.36, OC1 1034), whereas in fact he had resorted to the not uncommon practice of consigning his offspring – five in all – to the home for foundlings. Perhaps Rousseau did not see in the question an invitation to sacrifice himself for truth. But more plausibly, he perhaps could not easily come to terms with the question, even with truth at stake, for he can only offer some rather weak remarks about how he should have upbraided the young lady for the indiscretion of her question rather than replying to it as he did. And we shall find that in a later promenade he returns with considerable unease to his behavior as a father.

After these acknowledgements of his lies, he turns to the *Confessions* and to the aversion for falsehood that manifested itself most strongly in his intention to portray himself. And he relates two events that he chose not to include there, in both of which he suffered from the fault of another, preferring to "remain more assiduously silent about the good than about the evil." (CW8.37, OC1.1036) These bring him to another ostensible conclusion, that "the commitment I made to truthfulness is founded more on feelings of uprightness and equity than on the reality of things." (CW8.39, OC1.1038) But is this enough, for the man who took as his motto *Vitam impendere vero*? Rousseau thinks not. He should have sacrificed, not merely his interest, but also his weakness and timidity, "never to let fictions or fables come out of a mouth and a pen which had been specifically consecrated to the truth."

(CW8.40, OC1.1039) Yet the puzzle should remain. To resolve it, we should see Rousseau's dedication to truth rather differently, in the light of the note at the beginning of the Geneva manuscript of the *Confessions*. "Here is the only portrait of a man, painted exactly according to nature and in all its truth, that exists and that will probably ever exist." (CW5.3, OC1.3) Rousseau sought the truth of a portrait. The *Confessions* and the *Reveries* are his canvasses; what he painted on those canvasses is intended to reveal the true man. His truthfulness has its foundation, neither in moral sentiments nor in the reality of things, but in the demand to reveal his own nature. We must ask if he succeeds, if his portrait is indeed painted in all nature's truth. Or is Jean-Jacques, like Émile and the Citizen, yet another illusion?

It may seem that Rousseau's nature is most fully revealed in the next of his promenades, an eloquent, profoundly moving retelling of his brief stay on the island of Saint-Pierre in the Swiss lake of Bienne. Indeed, so seductive is this reverie that I almost hesitate to listen to it, since it intimates a very different resolution to our quest – a quest both for Rousseau's true nature and for a redemptive vision – than I believe he ultimately reaches. But with this warning, let us hear Rousseau tell us that "[o]f all the places I have lived . . . none has made me so genuinely happy nor left me such tender regrets as the Island of Saint-Pierre[2] in the middle of Lake Bienne." (CW8.41, OC1.1040) And what brought him this happiness?

I set about doing the Flora petrinsularis and describing all the plants of the Island . . . in sufficient detail to occupy myself for the rest of my days. . . . As a result of this fine project, every morning after breakfast . . . I would go off, a magnifying glass in hand and my *Systema naturae* under my arm, to visit a district of the Island, which I had divided into small squares for this purpose, with the intention of covering them one after the other in each season. (CW8.43, OC1.1043)

[2] Tr., "St. Peter's Island."

Botanizing increasingly became Rousseau's passion as he grew older, and his encounters with plants brought him the peace and contentment he could not find among men.

So here on this little island, we shall join Rousseau in his botanizing. Effectively exiled from France and Geneva, he has come from Môtiers in the principality of Neuchâtel, where he had lived under the protection of its prince, the king of Prussia. But his views excited the wrath of the clergy, his house was stoned, and so he has fled to the island of Saint-Pierre. Despite his desire to remain, he will be refused asylum by the Bernese, in whose territory it lay, so that after a mere forty-three days he will be forced to move on – this time to England and his celebrated encounter with David Hume. But that lies in the future. Let us join him in the present. After his morning botanizing, Rousseau spends his afternoons idly, boating on the lake, visiting a smaller island lacking human habitation, but to which he has transported a colony of rabbits, or simply rambling about the larger island. In fine weather, as evening approaches he sits in a secluded spot on the shore, letting the sound of the waves still his soul. "The ebb and flow of this water," he tells us, "was enough to make me feel my existence with pleasure and without taking the trouble to think." (CW8.45, OC1.1045) Has he returned to the condition of the earliest human, whose "first sentiment was that of his existence"? (CW3.43, OC3.164)

He recalls those evenings.

But if there is a state in which the soul finds a solid enough base to rest itself on entirely and to gather its whole being into, without needing to recall the past or encroach upon the future; in which time is nothing for it; in which the present lasts forever without, however, making its duration noticed and without any trace of time's passage; without any other sentiment of deprivation or of enjoyment, pleasure or pain, desire or fear, except that alone of our existence, and having this sentiment alone fill it completely; as long as this state lasts, he who finds himself in it can call himself happy, not with an imperfect, poor, and relative happiness such as one finds in the pleasures of life, but with a sufficient, perfect, and full happiness which leaves in the soul no emptiness it might feel a need to fill. Such is the state in which I often found myself during my solitary reveries on the Island of Saint-Pierre,[3] either lying in my boat as I let it drift with the water or seated on the banks of the tossing lake; or elsewhere, at the edge of a beautiful river or of a brook murmuring over pebbles. (CW8.46, OC1.1046–7)

Without "any other sentiment . . . except that alone of our existence." Prior to all thought, to all reflection, this sentiment fills the solitary condition in which humankind originates. It seems to be the sole innate sentiment, as all others originate in the experiences that force each person into awareness of a world independent of her and that sets the conditions for her preservation. In society, this sentiment becomes transformed into one of dependence, whether on one's recognition by the alien wills of other individuals, or on one's acceptance into the collective body of citizens under the direction of the general will. But for Rousseau on the island of Saint-Pierre, this sentiment has returned to its origin in solitude.

"What do we enjoy in such a situation?" Rousseau asks. And he answers,

Nothing external to ourselves, nothing if not ourselves and our own existence. As long as this state lasts, we are sufficient unto ourselves, like God. The sentiment of existence stripped of any other emotion, is in itself a precious sentiment of contentment and of peace which alone would suffice to make this existence dear and sweet to anyone able to spurn all the sensual and earthly impressions which incessantly come to distract us from it and to trouble its sweetness here-below. (CW8.46, OC1.1047)

But this paean is not Rousseau's final word. Recall that "absolute solitude is a state that is sad and contrary to nature," and that "our true *self* is not entirely within us." Rousseau experienced true happiness on the island of Saint-Pierre, but it is not the final

[3] Ibid.

happiness that he has yet to recall. Madame de Warens still waits to reenter the *Reveries.*

The beauty and power of the fifth promenade suggest a reading of the *Reveries* that would make it the centerpiece, conveying Rousseau's final recognition that he was indeed the solitary walker. However we interpret the *Reveries*, the rebirth of the second promenade provides Rousseau with a new starting point from which to answer his question, "What am I myself?" The third promenade licenses Rousseau's metaphysics; the fourth provides an interpretation of his motto that underlies his attempt to paint the true portrait of himself. The fifth then provides that portrait, and the remaining walks may be expected to add detail to the picture, to reinforce the answer and to refute alternative answers. And were it not for the final promenade, this would suggest a very plausible reading of the *Reveries.* But I shall argue that the seventh walk points in a different direction, and that the final promenade, in which love reenters Rousseau's account of himself, changes everything. It confirms instead Rousseau's remark in the *Dialogues,* a remark clearly incompatible with understanding Jean-Jacques as the solitary. Nevertheless, there is a bliss in solitude, and we must do it justice in our account.

And from that bliss of solitude Rousseau turns to the strain of society. The sixth promenade provides his clearest response to the idea of "Citizen of Geneva," although the Citizen is never mentioned by name. But Rousseau's judgment is unequivocal:

I have never been truly suited for civil society where everything is annoyance, obligation, and duty and . . . my independent natural temperament always made me incapable of the subjection necessary to anyone who wants to live among men. As long as I act freely, I am good and do only good. But as soon as I feel the yoke either of necessity or of men, I become rebellious, or rather, recalcitrant; then I am worthless.[4] (CW8.56, OC1.1059)

[4] Tr., "ineffectual"; Fr. "*nul.*"

How does Rousseau reach the conclusion that he is unfit for society? The sixth promenade begins with a brief story. Near the Porte d'Enfer a woman has a vending stall; her crippled son begs pleasantly from passers-by. When first he walked this way, Rousseau happily gave the boy money, but as time passed, "[t]his pleasure, having gradually become a habit, was inexplicably transformed into a kind of duty I soon felt to be annoying." (CW8.49, OC1.1050) Rousseau realizes that he changed his route to avoid the lad. He now recognizes this as an instance of his rebellion against any feeling of constraint. Even should it at first harmonize with his desire, in time it turns the desire to repugnance. And he relates his subjection to law: "But when the one who has received it . . . makes it a law for me to be his benefactor forever for my having at first taken pleasure in helping him, from that point annoyance begins." (CW8.51, OC1.1053)

Not only law but also contract enters his account.

I know that there is a kind of contract, and even the holiest of all, between the benefactor and the beneficiary. They form a sort of society with each other, more restricted than the one which unites men in general. And if the beneficiary tacitly pledges himself to gratitude, the benefactor likewise pledges himself to preserve for the other, as long as he does not make himself unworthy of it, the same good will he has just shown him and to renew its acts for him whenever he is able to and whenever it is required. (CW8.52, OC1 1053–4)

One may refuse to confer an initial favor, but having once given, then "[i]n this refusal, one feels[5] an inexplicable injustice and greater harshness than in the other; but it is no less the effect of an independence the heart loves and renounces only with effort." (CW8.52, OC1.1054)

In his discussion Rousseau points, not to the abuses of society, but to its legitimate features. There is no suggestion that his unfitness for society results from his unwillingness to bow to the

5 Tr., "we feel"; Fr. "*on sent.*"

sway of an unbridled *amour propre* that enslaves each to the opinions of his fellows. Rather, it results from the presence of obligation and duty – from those features central to the moral transformation that humans experience in entering society. Recall Rousseau's insistence, in the *Social Contract*, that "the voice of duty replaces physical impulse and right replaces appetite" (CW4.141, OC3.364), and again, in the *Political Economy*, that "since one shares the rights of citizens at birth, the instant of our birth should be the beginning of the performance of our duties." (CW3.155, OC3.260) But here in the *Reveries* Rousseau rejects duty; he insists that "to take all the delight in a good act away from me, it was sufficient for it to become a duty for me." (CW8.51, OC1.1052) And in rejecting duty, Rousseau is implicitly rejecting citizenship. He is refusing to substitute the general will for his own private will. He has claimed that legitimate society rests on a contract in which "as each gives himself to all, he gives himself to no one" (CW4.139, OC3.361), and, sharing the sovereign general will, "nevertheless obeys only himself and remains as free as before." (CW4.138, OC3.360) But one gives oneself to constraint, to obligation and duty, and for Rousseau this is always experienced as subjection. Calling it *liberty*, as Rousseau does in his political writings, only conceals the constraint. There can be no way of uniting with others in civil society that leaves him with the sense of liberty, of free existence, that he enjoys in his independent, solitary, natural condition.

Rousseau is the Citizen in absentia. In the dedicatory paean to Geneva that accompanies the *Discourse on Inequality*, he may have seen himself as "uselessly regretting the repose and Peace of which my imprudent youth deprived me" (CW3.6, OC3.115), but the deprivation is the basis of his real existence. Locked outside Geneva's gates, he had resolved never to return, and when he did return, officially to resume the faith and the citizenship he had cast off, it was only to leave again, this time forever. To be a Citizen, by his own standards of citizenship, Rousseau would have had to be a real part of the people he deemed sovereign. He would have had to sense his own existence as an inseparable part of their communal whole. Rousseau saw his dedication to truth as requiring him to be the Citizen, but he could take on no more than the name. Just as in his guise as Vaussore de Villeneuve he was exposed by those who knew music, and when posing as Dudding he would have been exposed by anyone who understood a few words of English, so the Citizen would have been exposed by anyone who understood the requirements of the role. And as Diderot's remark quoted in the preceding chapter makes clear, the incongruity of a citizen in absentia was not lost on his fellows. Not all of Rousseau's associates accepted his sincerity.

Did Rousseau come to see this? When he acknowledged that he had "never been truly suited for civil society where everything is annoyance, obligation, and duty" (CW8.56, OC1.1059), and that "my independent natural temperament always made me incapable of the subjection necessary to anyone who wants to live among men" (ibid.), did he recognize that he was repudiating his claim to be, or to have been, the Citizen? Here we are asking about Rousseau's understanding of his own personal truth, but we may look beyond this to the larger but not unrelated truth of his doctrine. In recognizing his own unfitness for civil society, did he not acknowledge, explicitly or implicitly, the unfitness of human beings for his ideal of citizenship? In assuming the role of Citizen, did Rousseau not license himself to promulgate a doctrine that his true self denies? We have yet to find the answer to Rousseau's question, "What am I myself?"; but in finding that it is not "Citizen of Geneva," have we not also found that saying *aidons-nous* does not lead to the recovery of the freedom lost when we began to say *aidez-moi*?

We have seen Rousseau write of benefactor and beneficiary as forming "a sort of society." In responding to the plea "Help me!" the benefactor in effect creates a kind of collectivity, an "us" to which he is now bound. When it replaces the recurrent individual pleas for help with the larger society of mutual assistance, *aidons-nous* transforms the particular bonds that constrain each benefactor into the universal bond that now defines each member of society, who senses his existence only in relation to the whole. This transformation yields, not freedom, but total constraint.

If we read the fifth promenade as Rousseau's discovery of himself as a solitary, then the sixth is its natural complement, Rousseau's discovery of himself as not a social being, not a citizen. Together the two would propound the main theses of the *Reveries*, accepting one answer, and denying another, to the initial question, "What am I myself?" But even if the solitary is not Rousseau's final truth about himself, the rejection of the social, as the realm of duty and obligation, and so of citizenship, still stands. We know now what Rousseau is not.

"The collection of my long dreams is scarcely begun, and I already feel it is near its end. Another pastime takes its place, absorbs me, and even deprives me of the time to dream." (CW8.57, OC1 1060) We have already been introduced to this other pastime on the island of Saint-Pierre. Botanizing came to be Rousseau's preoccupation. The world of plants provided a refuge for the solitary walker. Much of the seventh promenade, whose beginning I have just quoted, recalls why he developed an interest in botanizing, and explains the particular characteristics of this interest. But toward the end he turns to "a botanical[6] excursion I will remember all my life . . . near the Robaila" (CW8.65, OC1.1070, order transposed), a mountain farm in the principality of Neuchâtel. And in this expedition we shall find a remark that dissolves what may seem the finely crafted picture in the preceding promenades of the asocial solitary.

"I went deep into the winding crevices of the mountain; . . . I arrived at a retreat so hidden that I have never seen a more

---

[6] Tr., "plant."

desolate sight." (CW8.65, OC1.1070) Rousseau describes the trees – black fir and beech – the birds he heard or saw, the plants "which charmed and absorbed me for a long time. But gradually overcome[7] by the strong impression of the surrounding objects, I forgot botany and plants . . . and began to dream more at ease thinking that I was in a refuge unknown to the whole universe." (CW8.66, OC1.1071) Safe now from his enemies, he began to feel pride. Comparing himself to "those great travelers who discover an uninhabited Island," he said to himself, "'Without a doubt, I am the first mortal to have penetrated to this place'." [8] (Ibid.) Is this the reaffirmation of the solitary?

A familiar clanking from not far off interrupted his reverie. "I . . . burst through a thicket of brush . . . , and, in a little hollow twenty paces[9] from the very place where I believed myself to have been the first to arrive, I saw a stocking mill." (CW8.66, OC1.1071) What must interest us is "the confused and contradictory agitation I felt in my heart at this discovery. My first impulse was a feeling of joy to find myself back among humans when I had believed myself totally alone." (Ibid.) Although this gave way to the distress of "being unable, even in the deepest recesses of the Alps, to escape from the cruel hands of men eager to torment me," this first reaction is deeply instructive, for it is not that of the solitary. Rather it is an admission that "our sweetest existence is relative and collective." (CW1.118, OC1.813) Although unfit for the constraints of civil society, Rousseau proclaimed himself at the outset of the *Reveries* as "the most sociable and the most loving of humans." (CW8.3, OC1.995) As we read in the *Confessions*, "To be loved by everyone who approached me was my keenest desire." (CW5.12, OC1.14) Botanizing on the Robaila, he finds joy in the very presence of humans. But in a world in which he

---

[7] Tr., "imperceptibly dominated"; Fr. "*insensiblement dominé.*"

[8] Tr., "thus far."

[9] Tr., "feet"; Fr. "*pas.*"

is, or believes himself, the object of universal hatred rather than of affection, this joy cannot be sustained. Sociable but not social, solitary not by nature but through circumstance and in need of affection, Rousseau's self remains unresolved.

Rousseau makes no explicit attempt to link his promenades. But we might think that the "confused and contradictory agitation" he recalled from his botanical excursion prompts him to meditate "upon the dispositions of my soul during all the situations of my life" (CW8.69, OC1.1074) in the eighth promenade. And he finds that quite contrary to what one might expect, he "savored the sweetness of existence more, . . . really lived more" when he was in adversity – or what he believed to be adversity – rather than when he took all to be well. "When all was in order around me . . . [m]y expansive soul extended itself to other objects. . . . I was entirely devoted to what was alien to me." (Ibid.) Adversity has enabled him to recover his sense of self. The key step in this recovery, as he recognizes, is the reconversion of *amour propre* into *amour de soi*. The initial conversion of *amour de soi* into *amour propre* transformed humans from solitary to social beings. The reverse transformation has taken Rousseau back into solitude. His own *amour propre*, first curbed by what he took to be his terrible discovery of the plot against him, has been severed from all those links with other persons that fuel its demands for recognition and priority. And so it has once more become *amour de soi*, returning "to the natural order" and freeing Rousseau "from the yoke of opinion." (CW8.73, OC1.1079) With this thought he is finally released to "take pleasure in [his] own self in spite of" his enemies. (OC1.1084, my trans.)[10] He no longer seeks the help or the love of his fellows; he no longer speaks the words "Help me!" or "Love me!" But as we are soon to find, love remains at the core of his being, and at the center of his enjoyment of his own existence.

---

[10] Butterworth (CW8.77) translates *"jouis de moi même"* simply as "enjoy myself."

There is yet one part of his life that he must try to exorcise, if he is to taste this enjoyment. "I had placed my children in the foundling home. This was enough to let them [his enemies] misrepresent me as a denatured father; and from that, pushing and pulling this idea, they had little by little drawn the consequence that I evidently hated children." (CW8.79, OC1.1086) We need not pursue the details of Rousseau's unconvincing rationalizations of his paternal behavior, but we do need to consider his view of his relationships with children. "If I have made any progress in understanding the human heart, it is the pleasure I used to take in seeing and observing children." (CW8.80, OC1.1087) He recounts some of these experiences; one is particularly illuminating.

One evening, in the company of his wife,[11] Rousseau was sitting in the shade in the gardens of La Muette when a group of some twenty little girls with a governess settled nearby. At this point an "*oublieur*" came on the scene – a man who might best be described as selling chances on sweet wafers; one paid to draw a ticket that then determined how many wafers one would receive. Some of the girls had money and wanted to buy. When the governess hesitated, Rousseau offered to pay for all the girls to have a chance. "There were no blanks and at least one wafer came to each . . .; but to make the party still gayer, I secretly told the waferman to use his ordinary skill in an opposite sense by making as many good spins as possible occur and that I would make it up to him." (CW8.82–3, OC1.1091) Rousseau's behavior is hardly open to criticism, and yet are we not in the presence of the Tutor, arranging the "little scene" with the magician and the duck?

"[T]hat afternoon was one of those of my life which I remember with the greatest satisfaction." (CW8.83, OC1.1091) We should not want to deny Rousseau such satisfaction, but we need to be aware of the means by which it is attained. The man who

---

[11] In the *Reveries*, as in the *Confessions*, Thérèse is a marginal presence.

arranges matters so that others will take themselves to be the beneficiaries of good fortune is also the man who believes that others arrange matters so that he will seem to be the victim of ill fortune. His continued reflections in the ninth promenade bring him back to his ever-present awareness of his estrangement from his fellows. He has gained what perspective he can on his ills, both past and present. So "what am I myself?"

"Today, Palm Sunday, it is precisely fifty years since I first met Mme de Warens." (CW8.89, OC1.1098) With Rousseau, we return from 1778 to 1728, to "this first moment [that] determined my whole life. . . . My soul, whose most precious faculties my organs had not developed, still had no fixed form." (Ibid.) As we know, she sent him away, but everything called him back, and "for a long time yet before possessing her, I only lived in her and for her."[12] (Ibid.) "There is not a day," he affirms, "when I do not recall[13] with joy and tenderness this unique and brief time of my life when I was myself, fully, without admixture and without obstacle, and when I can genuinely say that I lived." (CW8.89, OC1.1098–9) In the ninth book of the *Confessions*, Rousseau saw himself with "a naturally expansive soul for which to live was to love. . . . Devoured with the need to love without ever having been able to satisfy it very well, I saw myself . . . dying without having lived." (CW5.358, OC1.426) But as he has told us in the eighth promenade, his "expansive soul" carried him outside himself, and now he recognizes the deep satisfaction of the "essential possession" that transforms love.

As Rousseau comes to his final understanding of himself, he juxtaposes two claims, "I only lived in her and for her" and "I was myself, fully." The imbalance of capacity and desire that is at the root of our fallen condition drops away. What Jean-Jacques would be no longer took him beyond what he actually was – "loved by

[12] Tr., "I only lived in and for her"; Fr. "*je ne vivais plus qu'en elle et pour elle.*"
[13] Tr., "No day passes but what I recall"; Fr. "*Il n'y a pas du jour où je ne me rappelle.*"

a woman full of desire to please and of gentleness, I did what I wanted to do, I was what I wanted to be; and . . . aided by her lessons and example, I was able to give to my still simple and new soul the form which better suited it and which it has always kept." (CW8.89–90, OC1.1099) And this form is that of the lover, not the solitary.

But the words "in her and for her" may give us pause. We are reminded of Pygmalion, living only through Galatea. Recall our question in Chapter 5 – does Jean-Jacques' identification with Madame de Warens involve an abnegation of self parallel to Pygmalion's? A negative answer emerges, not so much from any difference between "in" and "for" on the one hand, and "through" on the other, but from the difference in the contexts in which Jean-Jacques and Pygmalion make their claims. Jean-Jacques insists that his identification with his *maman* enables him to be fully himself. He does not lose himself in Madame de Warens but puts his existence in common with hers, so that, as he says in the *Confessions*, they become "*reciprocally* not only necessary but sufficient for each other." (CW5.186, emphasis mine, OC1.222). Pygmalion, on the other hand, keeps his existence distinct from Galatea only "to wish to be her" (OC2.1228), so that as she touches him, she senses only herself. There is no reciprocity between them, no common existence that they share. Jean-Jacques is not Pygmalion.

In acknowledging the effects of *maman*'s love, and her teaching and example, Rousseau is reiterating his recognition, in the *Confessions*, that he "became completely her work." (CW5.186, OC1.222) This might suggest that Jean-Jacques is Galatea, and Madame de Warens his maker, Pygmalion. But Rousseau never suggests that *maman* lives only to wish to be *petit*; what she has made is a lover with whom she can, in Rousseau's account, put her existence in common.

Rousseau's claim to be *maman*'s work does, however, seem to contradict the statement in the *Dialogues*, made by the character

Rousseau, that "[h]e [Jean-Jacques] is what nature made him. Education has changed him very little." (CW1.107, OC1.799) If Rousseau's nature is indeed that of the lover, and if that nature was realized through her work, then he is not what nature made him but what the education of his sentiments has achieved. But the Jean-Jacques of whom the character Rousseau speaks in the *Dialogues* is not the person who lived with Madame de Warens at Les Charmettes, but the very different person who has been forced unwillingly into solitude by his experiences of persecution. That person has indeed reverted to the natural solitariness of human nature, a condition unaffected by education. What the *Reveries* reveal, as the *Dialogues* do not, is the unnaturalness of this condition for the Jean-Jacques for whom "to live was to love." (CW5.358, OC1.426)

Rousseau's final memory is of freedom. "I could not bear subjection; I was perfectly free and better than free, for bound only by my affections, I did only what I wanted to do." (CW8.90, OC1.1099) In the *Social Contract* Rousseau had claimed that "the impulse of appetite alone is slavery, and obedience to the law one has prescribed for oneself is freedom." (CW4.142, OC3.365) But beyond both the rule of appetite and the rule of law, he has found the rule of affection. If the first is slavery and the second freedom, then the rule of affection is better than freedom.

Here, in his account of life with his beloved *maman* at Les Charmettes, we understand his telling us that our sweetest existence is relative, and our true self not entirely within us. Rousseau has freed himself from the chains of society, chains forged by need for the help of one's fellows. But he has not, cannot, would not free himself from the chains forged by love for one's fellows. Not only are these chains necessary to *be* one's true self, they are also necessary to *know* that self. "Without this short but precious time, I would perhaps have remained uncertain about myself. For, . . . all the rest of my life, I have been so troubled, tossed about, plagued by the passions of others that . . . I would have

difficulty unraveling what there is of my own in my own conduct."
(CW8.89, OC1.1099)

At the end of his life, Rousseau has recreated its true beginning. And we are now in a position to relate his creation of himself
to his other creations, Émile and the Citizen. In the *Social Contract* Rousseau poses the overarching problem that his political
writings address. There he seeks a kind of association combining the resources of its members while leaving each obedient to
himself alone and as free as before. More generally, we may say
that he seeks a form of life that will be sufficient, meeting the
needs of those it embraces, while leaving each his own master,
obedient to his own will, and so free. We began with natural man,
free because he is able to provide for his few needs through his
own efforts. Even reproduction demands no more than chance
encounter, willing copulation, easy childbirth, and rapid matu-
ration – and if this seems too quick a way of making the mother's
cares vanish, we should acknowledge once again that Rousseau
is never too scrupulous about taking the burdens of women into
his account. Natural man is free because he is unaware of all that
would enslave him. But gradually this awareness develops, and
with it the new needs and desires that lead each to seek the assistance of his fellows and so become dependent on their wills if
these new needs are to be met. We saw that implicit in the physical dependence entailed by the emergence of a division of labor,
beginning with cultivators and craftsmen, is the deeper psychological dependence of each on the other's favors. Each seeks
to be foremost, master of his fellow's wills, but Rousseau recognizes that mastery and servitude involve a mutual dependence in
which each comes to be only what the other acknowledges him
to be.

With freedom lost, we have undertaken, with Rousseau, the
quest for freedom regained. And we have at last come to the cul-
mination of that quest, in the young Jean-Jacques, the little one
who is lover and beloved of his *maman*, and who, a half-century

later, is described as "perfectly free and better than free." Jean-Jacques has found a life sufficient to his needs and desires, his need for "a [female] friend suited to [his] heart" (CW8.90, OC1.1099), his desire to be loved.[14] He does only what he would do. But so does Émile, and so, if the Legislator is successful, does the Citizen. Is Rousseau not dependent on Madame de Warens, as Émile on the Tutor, the Citizen on the Legislator? Rousseau does not deny this – quite the opposite. He sees himself as doubly dependent – dependent for his nature, the shaping of his soul, and dependent for his sentiment of existence, found in mutual possession. In the fifth chapter I called attention to Jean-Jacques' passivity in attaining the bliss of mutual possession. Freedom can be regained, whether for Rousseau, or Émile, or the Citizen, only if nature is appropriately shaped. Only by putting himself in Madame de Warens' hands, by acknowledging her as *maman*, can Jean-Jacques realize his true nature. Without her, he would be as powerless to resist being tossed and turned by the passions of others as, without the interventions of the Tutor, Émile would be powerless to resist the pressures of society, or, without the molding of the Legislator, the Citizen would be powerless to overcome the headlong rush to mutual enslavement. Freedom, for Rousseau, is never freely achieved.

But in considering Émile and the Citizen, I have questioned whether freedom is genuinely achieved, or even whether Rousseau, in his deepest self, believes that it is genuinely achieved. Is this true also of Jean-Jacques? The parallel between

[14] Here again Rousseau contradicts the passage in the ninth book of the *Confessions* to which I made reference earlier, since there he says, "I had not found a friend entirely my own." (CW5.358, OC1.426) Now he recognizes that Madame de Warens was that friend. But of course the friendship did not endure, and the passage in the *Confessions* anticipates his infatuation with Sophie, Comtesse d'Houdetot, who, being the lover of another man, was in fact anything but a "friend entirely my own." Sophie is never mentioned in the *Reveries*, and so plays no part in Rousseau's final quest for self-understanding.

the role played by Madame de Warens and the roles of Tutor and the Legislator should not lead us to overlook a fundamental difference. The Tutor and the Legislator are external to the freedom they seek to bring about. Émile's freedom is expressed in his relationship not with the Tutor, but with other persons; the Citizen's freedom is expressed in his relationship not with the Legislator, but with his fellow citizens. But Madame de Warens shapes Rousseau so that the two come to share their existence in common. She is, we might say, internally related to Jean-Jacques' freedom.

Rousseau has both withheld and conferred the label of love on his relationship with Madame de Warens. I have interpreted his thought by distinguishing two levels of love, the desire to possess another and its transformation into the will to identify with that other. I want to suggest that freedom undergoes a parallel transformation. Rousseau describes his younger self as "perfectly free and better than free." What is it to be better than free? We have seen that for Rousseau freedom is a condition of physical and psychological self-sufficiency. Natural man is free because his powers are adequate to his needs, and his sense of existence is self-contained. But he is free only because he is unaware of his limitations, and in particular of his lack of affections. Jean-Jacques' affections have been developed, but without alienating his sense of self. He enjoys a richer condition, better than free because he comes to exist only in and for another with whom his existence is merged, so that existing only in and for her, he exists only in and for his truest self.

"Ah! if I had sufficed for her heart as she sufficed for mine." (CW8.89, OC1.1098) But as we learned in our reading of the *Confessions*, he did not; he found his place taken. In the final promenade, however, Jean-Jacques is not supplanted.

My only worry was the fear it [his sweet state] might not last for long; and this fear, born of the instability of our situation, was not without foundation. From then on I thought about how to take my mind off this worry. . . . I thought that a provision of talents was the surest resource against misery, and I resolved to use my leisure to put myself in a position, if it were possible, to give back one day to the best of women the help I had received from her. (CW8.90, OC1.1099)

And here Rousseau pauses, never to resume.

When he had returned to Madame de Warens after she had first dispatched him to Turin, he had set out with a Hiero-fountain, convinced that it would make his fortune. It made him not a penny. Now, he relates at the end of the first part of the *Confessions*, "I left Savoy with my System of music, as I had formerly left Turin with my Hiero-fountain." (CW5.228, OC1.272) The comparison is just, but his intent in parting is clear. He still lives in and for his *maman*, but he can no longer live with her; he will therefore give his departure direction by becoming a knight in her service. In the last words of the *Reveries* he begins to recall this. And then there is silence. Soon after, he is dead. He has rediscovered his true nature, but it exists for him only in an unfinished recollection. Yet this recollection "covers with its charm everything dreadful in my present lot." (CW8.90, OC1.1099) The union of lover and beloved is precarious, fleeting, but the epiphany of love illuminates all that succeeds it. So is the quest complete? In being "better than free," is freedom regained?

Between solitude and society Rousseau has placed the power of love. True love is an exclusive relationship, in which the souls of the lovers merge into a single, sufficient whole. It does not invite the "expansive soul" to extend "itself to other objects" (CW8.69, OC1.1074), but instead is filled with "affectionate feelings" that "nourish the soul." (CW1.118, OC1.813) The lover avoids the sad state of absolute solitude, but avoids equally putting his being into things that are alien to him. The lover's true self is not altogether within himself but in union with his beloved. Should we then think that, in the last of his promenades, Rousseau has reached a truth at once personal and political? It is personal in revealing his true nature as formed by Madame de Warens' response to his demand to be loved, so that he was "completely her work," and as expressed in them coming to "put [their] whole existence in common." But it is also political, in rejecting both the individualism of the self-sufficient man that Rousseau examines in *Émile*, and the collectivism of the self-sufficient community that he examines in the *Social Contract* and the *Political Economy*, in favor of what we might call a dualism, in which love grounds a substantive union of man and woman as complementary individuals. Should we take this idea and ideal of substantive union as Rousseau's true legacy to political and social understanding? Is the complex interplay that he traces of love, freedom, and the sentiment of existence, the answer to the self-alienation that Rousseau reveals to be ubiquitous in modern life?

But love does not endure. Rousseau's last word is "*reçue.*" He has received, but there is no repayment. To continue would reveal the illusion. The incompleteness of the last promenade marks the point at which "the only portrait of a man, painted exactly according to nature and in all its truth" would cease to show the image of a man who, through the magic of *aimez-moi*, had come to be "better than free." So should we conclude rather with the thought that Rousseau, after all, presents the Tutor's view of love? Has he created another universe, inhabited with a Jean-Jacques and a Madame de Warens who exist only within it, sharing the illusion that love creates? Rousseau charms us; he depicts the young Émile in the care of the Tutor, the citizens of an idealized Geneva, the solitary on the island of Saint-Pierre, Jean-Jacques and his *maman* at Les Charmettes – and the beauty and force of each picture invite us to share the world it depicts. His dreams speak to many of our deepest feelings; but awakening, we see that Émile is the manipulated creature of his Tutor, that true citizens would be the denatured products of the Legislator, that the solitary is alienated from all humankind, that Rousseau and

Madame de Warens fail to sustain, if ever they really enjoyed, the idyll of love.

Rousseau does not accompany us to the last of these awakenings. Jean-Jacques has received, and to have received is not to have failed. At the outset of the *Confessions* Rousseau came to us, "this book in my hands." In this inquiry I have read this and his other books, interrogating them about the truths they seek and the illusions they find. I have pursued them to their unfinished end, the last promenade when a further step would expose the illusion in *aimez-moi*, the cry with which all language begins. In not taking that further step Rousseau reveals the man who lived in these words, making their illusion his truth.

Index